Mastering
Self-Confidence
with NLP

Mastering Self-Confidence with NLP

Kerry Johnson, MBA, Ph.D.

MEDIA

Published 2019 by Gildan Media LLC
aka G&D Media
www.GandDmedia.com

FIRST EDITION 2019

Front Cover design by David Rheinhardt of Pyrographx

Interior design by Meghan Day Healey of Story Horse, LLC

Library of Congress Cataloging-in-Publication Data is available upon request

ISBN: 978-1-7225-0183-9

10   9   8   7   6   5   4   3   2   1

Contents

One

Why Do You Need Self-Confidence?

Are you self-confident? Do you wonder whether you will be able to complete a task effectively? Do you get nervous during a performance? Do you feel anxiety in sports, business, or even on stage? If you are like a lot of people, you lack self-confidence at times. You sometimes worry if you will be able to complete a task, let alone be successful. You worry that your career and activities will suffer. You really want more out of your life, but aren't willing to take the risks you need to get there. The answer is to build your self-confidence.

Self-confidence does not merely imply belief in your ability to succeed. You are self-confident about many things, while others cause you stress. A lack of self-confidence often means that you dwell on the negative consequences of failing. But becoming more self-confident means that you can have more enjoyment and success in everything you do.

Many years ago, my daughter Catherine had to go through the long student-loan process to finish college. To say that she was stressed was an understatement. But if I did the loan application for her, not only would she not learn how to do it, she would not have been able to use the experience to develop the confidence that she could do it in the future. So you see, the more successes we can stack up in our life, the more self-confidence we will have in everything else we do.

One of my tennis buddies heard that I was writing a book on self-confidence. He said he had the answer: just win all the time. That will build up your self-confidence.

But in case you lose once in a while, like me, this book is for you.

Did you know that self-confident people make more money? Many studies show a link between high self-confidence and higher levels of income. Some studies have even shown that those who were confident earlier in school earned better wages and were promoted more quickly in their careers.

Much of self-confidence is about self-esteem. Self-esteem is directly connected to your social network. It's also about your activities and what you hear other people say about you. A positive level of self-esteem can be linked to your psychological and physical health, your body images, and whether you matter to people. Low self-esteem has been linked to depression, health problems, and antisocial behavior.

Your social and academic life impact your self-esteem. Your self-confidence and self-esteem also vary in different environments. While you may feel self-confident at home, you may lack self-confidence in your work.

In this book, you will learn about self-esteem and the attributes of someone with a lot of it. You will also learn about low self-esteem and behaviors showing false self-esteem, like narcissism, arrogance, and egotism. Next, you will learn about change and how difficult it is to modify any part of your personality, especially self-esteem and self-confidence. Only babies like change, yet your willingness to read this book shows that you are emotionally prepared to make the changes necessary to become much more self-confident.

Self-confidence is also about your ability to focus on pleasure instead of pain. Changing your mental state and thinking about the joy of completing a task and a pleasurable outcome will make you much more self-confident. But if instead you allow yourself to pay attention to a possible but improbable painful outcome, you will destroy self-confidence and harm your chances of success in the future.

Next we will talk about *locus of control*. This will help you understand whether your confidence comes from external things that happen to you, or whether you are able to control your environment. Are you internally controlled and confident? Or are you externally controlled, reactive to what happens around you? We will also help you develop self-efficacy, or your ability to be more effective in everything you do.

Many sports coaches believe that repetition can help you develop self-confidence. I think that's true. If you do something over and over again, you'll be confident in your ability to do things successfully. We aren't talking about false self-confidence, like trying to fly a 747 without any training. We're focusing on rational self-confidence, when you have to put in what one of my friends calls the "hard yards"—otherwise known as paying your dues.

But repetition, while important, needs to be matched also with goals and outcomes. We will talk about the difference between the two and why *experiencing* a goal is far better than just setting one.

A lack of self-confidence is usually displayed in anxiety and stress. Often we feel these negative emotions while participating in sporting events, stage performances, and speeches. This kind of stress is called *performance anxiety*. There are four fears we feel during performance anxiety: the fear of rejection, the fear of looking foolish, the fear of failure, and the fear of success.

Who would ever fear success? The problem is that many of us sabotage ourselves when we are too successful. This sounds very strange, but we will talk about how to manage and alleviate these fears, making it easier for you to develop a self-confident life.

There was a business executive who was deep in debt and could see no way out.

Creditors were closing in on him. Suppliers were demanding payment. He sat on the park bench, head in hands, wondering if anything could save his company from bankruptcy.

Suddenly an old man appeared before him. "I can see that something is troubling you," he said.

After listening to the executive's woes, the old man said, "I believe I can help you."

He asked the man his name, wrote out a check, and pushed it into his hand saying, "Take this money. Meet me here exactly one year from today, and you can pay me back at that time."

Then he turned and disappeared as quickly as he had come.

The executive saw in his hand a check for $500,000, signed by John D. Rockefeller, then one of the richest men in the world.

"I can erase my money worries in an instant!" the executive realized. But instead he decided to put the uncashed check in his safe. Just knowing it was there might give him the strength to work out a way to save his business, he thought.

With renewed optimism, he negotiated better deals and extended terms of payment. He closed several big sales. Within a few months, he was out of debt and making money once again.

Exactly one year later, the executive returned to the park with the uncashed check. At the agreed-upon time, the old man appeared. But just as the executive was about to hand back the check and share his success story, a nurse came running up and grabbed the old man.

"I'm so glad I caught him!" she cried. "I hope he hasn't been bothering you. He's always escaping from the rest home and telling people he's John D. Rockefeller." And she led the old man away by the arm.

The astonished executive stood there, stunned. All year long he'd been wheeling and dealing, buying and selling, convinced he had half a million dollars behind him.

Suddenly he realized that it wasn't the money, real or imagined, that had turned his life around. It was his newfound self-confidence that gave him the power to achieve anything he went after.

That is what self-confidence is all about. It's like knowing you have $500,000 in your pocket to save you, but also knowing you will never have to cash the check. Wouldn't it be nice to have that kind of confidence?

In the next section, we will talk about learned helplessness. There are certain things that you are convinced you will fail at. In fact, after you fail, you will actually learn you can't win and will never attempt it again. Martin Seligman, a famous psychological researcher, discovered that you may self-limit, or avoid trying things you have failed at in the past.

You may have bought this book because you wanted to increase your self-confidence using neurolinguistic programming, or NLP.

Using NLP will help you develop more self-confidence, using techniques like recasting your visualizations. How you see things in the future can be changed. Through NLP, you can dissipate, and sometimes eliminate, fears and phobias. In this new and very effective approach, you will learn how to see yourself successful at everything you want to do.

Since your beliefs are critical to self-confidence, changing your negative beliefs into positive expectations is also important. To achieve this, we will focus on a technique called *frame of reference.*

Self-esteem and self-confidence are also governed by how you approach and avoid your dreams: you tend to approach the things you like and avoid the things you don't. The NLP technique we will use to help you through this process is called *metapatterns.*

A University of Chicago professor developed a very interesting concept called *flow.* In his research, he discovered that your skill level must meet the same level of challenge for you to feel successful. As you meet the challenge, there's a certain level of effortlessness, or flow, that makes you feel completely confident and joyful. This flow state is the kind of feeling you have when you win a tennis match or hit the best golf score of your life. We will also work on NLP techniques called *anchoring* and *circle of excellence.*

When we feel a lack of self-confidence, we also feel stress. You and I will spend some time talking about the types of stress you will encounter and how to measure it. To do this, you will learn the Subjective Unit of Discomfort, or SUDS, scale.

I once heard a very self-confident person say that he faked it till he made it. You and I will work on a technique close to this, called *modeling*—how to mirror a very self-confident person you look up to and make those attributes your own.

In my graduate studies, I researched a concept called *behavior modification*. The technical term is *operant conditioning theory*. We will use this concept to change your negative behaviors into ones that help you become the self-confident person you want to be. To keep you on track, we will also implement *behavioral contracts*, a way to keep yourself accountable in your quest to become more self-confident.

Nearly all the research on self-confidence indicates that the earlier you can learn to be self-confident, the more successful in life you will be. If you have kids, the time to develop self-confidence in them is now. Kids without self-confidence are vulnerable to peers who may introduce them to drugs, teen pregnancy, and crime. Kids with self-confidence are more prepared to say no to the harmful things they should avoid, and are less vulnerable to peer pressure. In chapter 9, we will look at your parenting style and see if it is focused on raising self-confident children.

In addition to helping you become self-confident, I will also show you ways you can develop self-confidence in other people. I'm sure you have family members and friends in whom you would like to see more self-confidence. I will show you techniques that you can use to behavior-shape these people into a higher level of self-confidence.

So we have a lot to cover. But we will also have a lot of fun. You will learn all the tools you need to become more self-confident and to apply them to everything you do in life. All you have to do is use the techniques you learn.

Self-Esteem

One component of self-confidence is self-esteem. While self-confidence is a belief in your ability to achieve an outcome, self-esteem is a reflection of your overall sense of self-worth. People with high self-esteem believe they are competent and worthy. In other words, self-esteem is your positive or negative emotional self-evaluation. One researcher defined *self-esteem* as *feeling worthy of happiness*. Another researcher, Nathaniel Branden, said that self-esteem is the sum of self-confidence and self-respect. You can think of self-esteem as your mental state and of self-confidence as your ability to face life's challenges successfully. This will help you possess the knowledge that whatever happens, you will be successful.

Here are some attributes of people with high self-esteem:

- You believe in certain values and principles. You are ready to defend them, even when finding opposition.
- You are able to act according to what you think is best, trusting your own judgment, and don't feel guilty when other people don't like your choices.
- You don't worry excessively about what happened in the past or what may happen in the future. You learn from the past, but you live intensively in the present.
- You trust in your capacity to solve problems, but when you have setbacks and difficulties, you are ready to ask others for help.
- You understand that you're interesting and valuable to other people, especially your friends.
- You resist manipulation, and you collaborate with others only if it's beneficial to both of you.
- You are able to enjoy a great variety of activities, not just the ones you do well.
- You can work toward finding solutions and voice disappointment without belittling yourself or other people when challenges occur.

As Winston Churchill once said, "pessimists see the difficulty in every opportunity. Optimists see the opportunity in every difficulty."

Low Self-Esteem and Narcissism

People with low self-esteem possess a number of negative attributes. They criticize themselves heavily and often seem very dissatisfied. They are hypersensitive to others and feel resentment when criticized, having almost a sense of being attacked. They have an excessive desire to please others, beyond being generous. They have neurotic guilt and dwell on past mistakes, and even increase the magnitude of those setbacks. In other words, they continue to beat themselves for past errors. People with low self-esteem also seem to be very pessimistic and have a generally negative outlook towards life. This is probably because they don't feel equipped with the emotional tools to face those challenges successfully.

One of the most debilitating aspects of low self-esteem is the tendency to see temporary setbacks as permanent. One of my clients wanted to sponsor me to speak to 2000 attendees at an investment conference in Canada. The conference organizer was able to secure a sponsor in competition with my client. I had to tell the client that his competitor locked up an exclusive sponsorship. My client said, "No problem; I know something good will arise from this." This is an example of someone who has such high self-esteem that he thinks success will come to him, no matter what the circumstances.

By contrast, people with low self-esteem see setbacks as debilitating and permanent. They would look at the conference setback as another reason they are unable to get any breaks in the world, and another reason they will never be really successful.

Types of Self-Esteem

There are two types of self-esteem: *implicit* and *explicit*. People with implicit self-esteem evaluate themselves unconsciously negatively or positively on the basis of how they *feel*. Those with explicit self-esteem incorporate more conscious and reflective self-evaluation: they evaluate themselves on the basis of what *happens* to them and their resulting self-talk—what they say to themselves. In any event, your self-esteem can be high or low, whether it is implicit or explicit. A good example is the character Eeyore from *Winnie-the-Pooh*. He always has a cloud over his head, no matter what happens. He has implicit self-esteem, but it is low.

Do you ever hear people say that you're negative? Do they ever ask, "Why are you always negative?" or say, "Just look at the positive?" If so, you may have implicit negative self-esteem. No matter what happens, you find a way to diminish good things, and you increase the importance of bad things that happen to you.

If, on the other hand, your self-esteem is implicit and positive, this is good, because it means that not much can steer you away from optimism.

People with explicit self-esteem react to what happens to them. You might hear someone tell you not to be so negative. Your response would be, "But look at what just happened to me! You would feel the same way!"

A related issue is narcissism. Narcissistic people have implicit self-esteem, but their self-worth is greatly inflated. They think their time and value are more important than those of anybody else. Their self-esteem isn't reactive to what happens to them; it is based on how they feel inside.

Egotism is a close relative of narcissism. An egotist will react in a hostile and aggressive way when their self-esteem is diminished. In contrast, a narcissist will simply devalue the critic. They will say things like, "What does he know? or "I would never listen to that guy—he's an idiot!"

I'm a tennis player. Most of my best friends are members of the Palisades Tennis Club in Newport Beach, California. I tend to cut loose at the club, teasing my friends, and act a lot more animated than I would at home or at work. I get teased a lot too. One of my friends introduced me as one of the smartest psychologists in the country—with his feet firmly planted in midair. I thought that was pretty funny. But about a year ago, one of my friends sat down with us after a few beers after a match. In front of four other friends, he said that he had just read a book on narcissism and saw me on every page. With my implicit level of self-esteem, I thought the author quoted me often in the book. But my buddy said he thought I was so narcissistic that the book described me perfectly. I was pretty shocked. Then one by one, all of my tennis buddies, probably drinking too much beer, lit into the critic, telling him that he knew nothing about narcissists. And they teasingly told him they were shocked that he could even read.

I am glad that my friends defended me, but I sometimes think that we mix up high degrees of self-confidence with narcissism and egotism. The difference is, those with high implicit positive self-esteem think of others as well as themselves, while narcissists think of only themselves.

Three States of Self-Esteem

There are three states of self-esteem: *shattered*, *vulnerable*, and *strong*.

Those with shattered self-esteem don't regard themselves as lovable or valuable. Sometimes they see themselves as defined by a single failure. For example, they may be plagued by a missed catch for a touchdown in a high-school championship football game. Or by failing a final test, killing their chances for medical school. Or in my case, by not being good enough to become a world-class tennis player (my dream when I was on the tennis tour in the seventies). A person with shattered self-esteem would let any one of those setbacks define themselves.

The person with *vulnerable* self-esteem actually could have positive levels of self-esteem, but it is vulnerable to the risk of something negative happening in the future—their business taking a downturn, an argument with a spouse, or even a lost sale that jeopardizes their income. These individuals use defense mechanisms like avoiding decisions. They may also blame other people in an effort to protect their self-image.

I saw an example of this many years ago when I was playing a tennis tournament. We were competing against another club. One of my friends was losing badly on another court. When I looked over, he was yelling at his opponent for hitting drop shots and lobs. He wasn't able to counter this player, so he started swearing at him, threw his racket, and walked off the court. This is an example of a self-esteem defense mechanism: "I won't play with you if I can't win."

Further proof of his low self-esteem occurred a few months ago when we spoke about friendship. He said he didn't have many friends. I said I considered him a good friend. He was truly surprised. On some level he may not have thought he deserved good friends.

People with *strong* self-esteem have such a highly positive self-image that life setbacks won't subdue them. They also have less fear of failure. They appear humble and cheerful, and can compete without worrying that their self-esteem will be affected. They don't worry as much about losing prestige or self-worth when they have setbacks. John McEnroe, the great tennis player of the 1980s, is now arguably the best tennis commentator on TV. The level of detail he gives to the game is extraordinary. That can only come from somebody who has played at an extremely high level. One of his most interesting comments about tennis pro Roger Federer is that Roger has a very short memory. When he hits a bad shot on the tennis court, he moves on quickly to the next point, forgetting his past mistake.

When I played doubles with a few of my friends last week, I lost three straight points by double-faulting. All I could think about during my next service game were my double faults. So guess what happened when I served again? I double-faulted. The greatest tennis players in the world, as well as other world-class athletes, forget their mistakes. As Tiger Woods once said after hitting a drive into the trees, "I need to chip my next shot onto the green." He could have said, "I hope I don't slice again. I will never be able to hit the ball straight again." Instead his memory evaporated. He only thought about the successful next shot. Great athletes are always thinking about the next shot instead of dwelling on the last bad one.

The same can be said of you. Can you think about your next achievement instead of dwelling on your last mistake?

Can You Change?

I have been talking for a while now about the types of self-esteem and self-confidence. At this point you may be asking yourself, "Can I really change my self-confidence and self-esteem?" The answer is yes and no. Before puberty, it's fairly easy to modify behavior. But after the age of twelve it's much more challenging. It will take you a lot longer to develop self-confidence and self-esteem as an adult than it will for your prepubescent kids.

Let me give you a couple of examples. The divorce rate for first marriages in America is 62 percent within ten years. When I speak, I usually ask a newlywed in my audience to stand up and tell me how long they have been married. I say, "How is your marriage going so far?" The group always laughs, because they have heard the "so far" part. I then jokingly ask if the newlywed has a prenup agreement. But I don't let them answer. It's usually too embarrassing.

What do you think the divorce rate is for second marriages in ten years? Higher or lower? If you guessed higher, you're right. It is 78 percent. The second-marriage divorce results from the same mistakes as the first marriage. I jokingly say that the reason is that you took yourself with you to the second marriage.

What do you think the divorce rate is for third marriages— higher or lower? Did you guess higher? Three strikes and you're out? You would be wrong. It's only 36 percent. Marriage counselors will tell you that after two failed marriages, people realize that it's not their partners' fault; they're the one they need to change.

Now if you realize how difficult change is, you must know that changing yourself from a pessimist to an optimist, from low self-esteem to high self-esteem, from low self-confidence to high self-confidence, is a monumental task. You can do it, but it will take consistency, dedication, and patience.

Here are three stages of change: *deny, resist,* and *adapt.*

Most people *deny* they need to change. They just go on with life, unwilling to sacrifice. But sometimes something monumental happens—like divorce, business failure, or another negative life event—that causes them to rethink. Those who *resist* try to convince themselves they can get by without changing; it's the other people who need to change instead.

The last phase of change is to *adapt.* Once you come to the realization that you are willing to change, and sacrifice, you usually wish you'd done it five years ago.

Here are three ways to adapt to change and implement the skills to become more self-confident: First, expect any change to be beneficial. This flies in the face of low self-esteem, where something new tends to be thought of as negative.

One of my friends is an orthodontist in Malibu, California. He saw the great basketball player Kobe Bryant in his office for braces. My friend has a very unique way of actually improving his patients' jawlines, and facial appearance, just with braces. He's a master at what he does. After he described this procedure to Kobe, the basketball player's first response was, "Will this help me play better basketball?" Kobe's singular focus on what was important also made him willing to make any change necessary to become better.

Second, expect change to create stress. Anytime you change any part of your attitude or personality, it will be uncomfortable. Change and discomfort create stress, and stress will cause you to avoid the discomfort—becoming very busy instead of successful. You may know some people who, when confronted with bad news, try to mask the discomfort by becoming very busy. They may start cleaning or tinkering. Any change you make, good or bad, will cause you to engage in avoidance behaviors. It doesn't address the issue, but it helps you avoid facing the stress.

I see this all the time in my coaching practice. A client's business might be failing. I give them three things to do during the next week and ask them to commit to the activities. But when I check in with them on our next coaching call, they say they became too busy to implement those activities. Their excuse usually is, they are too busy doing inconsequential activities, like answering emails, cleaning up the database, or even doing paperwork. I see this every week, at some point, in nearly every client.

Third, be doggedly persistent. Go just one more round. On February 25, 1964, Cassius Clay was fighting Sonny Liston for the heavyweight boxing championship of the world. Liston had an arm reach that was four inches longer than Clay's, and he was three inches taller. By the eighth round, Clay was getting pulverized by a much stronger and faster Liston. But Clay had a secret weapon: his manager, Angelo Dundee. Dundee realized his fighter was getting tired and demoralized. In fact it was so bad that Clay told him he was quitting the fight. But Dundee said, "Go one more round." Clay said no. But as soon as the bell rang, Dundee pulled the chair out from under him and gave him a push in the back, forcing him one step forward. As soon as that step was taken, Liston's corner threw in a towel, signifying that Liston gave up. Cassius Clay won the fight, later became Muhammad Ali, and the rest is history.

Going one more round created one of the best boxers in the world. As you try to make any changes from what you read in this book, promise yourself to go one more round.

Pleasure and Pain

Our self-confidence depends on the pleasure or pain we associate with certain activities. Indeed our tendency to avoid punishment and seek reward is the prime psychological motivation for everything we do. We work for rewards, including money, recognition, and status. We're polite to people because we want them to like us.

Our children often phone us from college not because they especially want to talk to us, but because they need money. My daughter Stacey was a freshman at James Madison University in Virginia, majoring in business and communications. She would call once or twice a week. I began suspecting her of calling only when she needed money. Once she called when I was in a rush. As soon as I heard her voice, I said, "How much do you want?" She became indignant that I thought she only called when she needed money. I apologized and listened to her talk about her week and about how much reading she had to do. After about twenty minutes, I told her I had to go to a meeting, and she sprang to the real point of the conversation: "Dad, I really need $200!"

I once mentioned to an audience the notion that we are primarily motivated to earn rewards and avoid punishment. A woman raised her hand and said, "That's not true. I am a United Way volunteer." I replied that she was a United Way volunteer because she found it personally rewarding.

Determining how we personally cope with the pleasure and pain of life is the first step toward using pleasure to our advantage and keeping our fear of pain under control. Understanding that will help implement self-confidence in your life. If you are pain-focused, your self-confidence will be challenged. If you are pleasure-focused, your self-confidence is increased. The difference is that pleasure-focused people are self-confident because they are drawn to pleasurable outcomes, while those who are pain-focused avoid painful results. If you approached a task expecting pleasure, wouldn't you start it with more self-confidence than if you expected pain?

Take the short quiz below to determine whether you're pleasure-focused or avoidance-of-pain-focused:

1. If you are in the middle of a project, will you spontaneously take time off for a friend (pleasure-focused), or do you feel compelled to stay and complete the project because you perceive that some kind of punishment will occur if you don't (avoidance-of-pain-focused)?

2. Do you eat only the foods you like best on your plate at dinner (pleasure-focused), or do you eat at least some of all the foods because you fear that if you don't, you might get sick (avoidance-of-pain-focused)?

3. Do you work on projects only at the last minute, when you are in a panic to get them done (pleasure-focused), or do you begin projects early so that there's no way you'll miss a deadline and get in trouble (avoidance-of-pain-focused)?

4. When you wake up in the morning, do you get up only when you hear a chiding voice inside your head (pleasure-focused), or do you typically arrive at work at 7:00 a.m., even though you're not a morning person, so you will be able to complete your work even if unexpected problems arise (avoidance-of-pain-focused)?

5. Do you tend to do a mediocre job on things you don't like so that you can get to the fun projects more quickly (pleasure-focused), or do you typically do a conscientious job on all

projects, even those you don't particularly care for, in order to avoid getting caught (avoidance-of-pain focused)?

It doesn't take much to learn if you are pleasure- or pain-focused. If you answered yes to the pleasure-focus questions more often than the ones focused on the avoidance of pain, you may be someone who is more attracted to pleasure. If your answers suggest that you tend more to the avoidance of pain, it may take more than rich rewards to achieve your goals; it may take a perceived threat or loss to get you moving.

Procrastination

Whether you're pleasure- or avoidance-of-pain-focused, like most individuals, you probably procrastinate from time to time. Why? We procrastinate when we perceive future pain. The most salient reasons for procrastination are avoiding discomfort, a feeling of insecurity that you don't have the information or skill to do the task, and the lack of confidence that you can be successful.

Have you ever put off finishing an assignment and, when it came due, told a white lie to gain more time to complete it? Have you ever shuffled paper around your desk instead of making an important phone call, watched a sitcom instead of reading to the kids, or spent time in the middle of your business day opening mail, even when you knew it would be more efficient to read it in the late afternoon or during lunch?

Usually we feel guilty about procrastination, but not only is it a negative behavior, it can also cost us money. Being late is a form of procrastination. Years ago, as an aspiring consultant, I was twenty minutes late to an appointment with a customer. This was before the days of cell phones. I couldn't call ahead and warn him, so I just showed up late. My customer entered the waiting room and told me that if I didn't have the courtesy of arriving on time, he wouldn't extend me the courtesy of seeing me. I learned my lesson on the spot, but it cost me thousands of dollars in revenue.

In your quest to become more self-confident, it is important to control procrastination. The more you procrastinate, the lower your self-control. If your self-control is low, your self-esteem and self-confidence will be low as well. Procrastination will also lower your self-confidence in future projects.

A few years ago, I was assigned a deadline for writing a book. When the publisher asked me if I could keep to the schedule, I said, "Sure." After all, I had about four months to do the outline and another month to come up with a rough draft. But as you might have guessed, I waited until the week before the outline deadline to even start the project. I then waited until three weeks before the rough-draft deadline to put pen to paper. The project was completed, but to this day I wonder what would have happened if I had given myself enough time to do the best job that I could.

As I procrastinated in beginning the project, I felt terrible. I knew I was capable of doing a great job, but I didn't give myself enough time to do it. I allowed myself to be fooled into thinking that as soon as I had done the research, I could start writing. The problem was, I even procrastinated doing the research.

Sometimes people engage in avoidance behaviors because of aversive conditioning. For example, if you've ever been thrown from a horse, you may have been conditioned by this experience to never ride again. Likewise, if you've ever been on a diet and failed, you may have been aversely conditioned to never diet again.

This is kind of like the boy visiting a blacksmith shop. Wandering around, he picked up a red-hot horseshoe and immediately dropped it. The blacksmith said, "Did that burn you, son?" The boy said, "No, sir, it just doesn't take me long to look at a horseshoe."

Whatever its origins, procrastination often keeps us from doing what we need—and, frequently, want—to do. Since it is really a result of focusing on the pain of a task instead of its benefits, why not simply restructure how we perceive pain and pleasure?

Here are three simple steps that can restructure your associations, moving your expectation of a given activity from pain to pleasure. Any activity will become less painful if you remember to follow these steps. These steps will also help you visualize doing a good job on a project and limiting your negative self-talk, another consequence of a painful expected result. If you can change your expectations from pain to pleasure, your self-confidence will increase dramatically.

Restructuring Your Associations

1. Make a picture, sound, or feeling representation of your goal. Try to experience the result of the task before you even start it. For example, try to visualize a clean garage instead of how much effort it will take to get it that way. Focus on how much easier it will be to find the things you need, park the car, or just move around without being hit in the head by unidentified falling objects.

2. Intensify your perception of the good experience until the prospect of completion brings a smile to your face. Continue to intensify your image of what you see, hear, and feel. Make the garage so bright that it is blindingly clean. That should make you smile, especially if you haven't touched it in years.

3. Drop everything and start the activity immediately. You don't have to complete it; just start it. Do enough to change your emotions. Straighten up one corner of the garage, then celebrate with a drink. Write a cover letter or an opening statement for a report, and then stop and reward yourself. Make one of those sales calls you've been putting off. After you do, have a cup of coffee as a reward.

One other extremely effective technique for overcoming procrastination is to use the four basic steps of planning, learning, observing, and engaging.

1. **Plan.** One of the most common ways you can sabotage yourself is by failing to plan a project. You have likely heard in the past that "inch by inch, anything's a cinch." The hardest part is the first inch. You can make that first inch easier if you sit down and make a game plan of the project you wish to complete. Suppose you have to give a speech two weeks from today. You wouldn't wait until the last day to start preparing (or would you?).

In the most desirable situation, you'd first plan the major portion of your talk. You'd think about the purpose and whom you'd be speaking to. Then you'd plug in the points that illustrate each idea. Next, you might put in some humorous stories to illuminate your concepts. You'd probably jot down some notes about where to search for additional information. You'd also schedule practice time in order to give your presentation a dry run.

Planning is easy in the context of a speech, but it helps to combat self-doubt and procrastination in other areas too. Once you start the process of making a plan, you'll find it much easier to complete what you've been putting off.

2. **Learn**. Write down what you will have to learn in order to complete the project. We often feel paralyzed and procrastinate because we don't know what to do first. Recently I was assigned the task of writing a series of articles for a major magazine. I wasn't as familiar with the topic as I would have liked, so as I planned out the project, I put a check mark next to the areas that needed more research. During the next few weeks, I found myself talking to many people about the topic, and even thought about it on my way to work in the morning. I spent time researching the issues I was confused about and noticed that most of my initial confusion simply evaporated.

This is a side benefit of planning early. On the flip side, if you wait to start any part of your project until the day it is due, you will not be able to let your mind automatically solve problems for you. It is said that Thomas Edison encountered huge problems in creating the light bulb. Often when he got stuck, he would leave his lab and take a short nap. When he awoke, he frequently had a solution to the problem.

3. **Observe**. What is it that keeps you from arriving on time to appointments? Or causes you to procrastinate on easy chores like balancing your checkbook? Take out a sheet of paper and list the emotional benefits you receive from procrastinating. If this sounds like a silly exercise, think again. I tried this to help solve my problem of tardiness and was surprised to learn that I have an intense loathing of waiting. The thought of sitting in someone's office reading a useless magazine causes me real irritation.

4. **Engage**. The last step in overcoming procrastination is to engage yourself in your goal. This simply means that you're attempting to start it. As mentioned earlier, simply by taking the first step, you

can get moving in the right direction. I have completed many major projects with the initial plan of doing only a few minutes of work. In every case, I've ended up completing the job.

The most productive achievers work a little each day on important projects, even if only to open a folder and review what they have done so far. If you engage yourself in doing something with a high degree of frequency, there is absolutely no way you will be able to put it off for long.

Locus of Control

Another aspect of becoming self-confident is your *locus of control*. This refers to whether you believe you can control events that affect you. This defines whether you are an *internal* person, meaning that you believe that you can control your life, or an *external* person, meaning that you believe that your decisions and your life are out of your control and happen by fate.

I know this seems a little like external and internal self-esteem, but it is different in the way that your believe that events in life affect you. If you have a strong internal locus of control, you believe events in your life happen because of your own actions. For example, your academic test scores are the result of your own ability and how much you studied. If your locus of control is external, you blame poor test scores on outside events, like a bad teacher or distractions in the classroom.

Locus of control is very important in developing self-confidence. If you have an external locus of control, that is, if you don't believe you can control an outcome, you also believe that confidence and self-esteem don't matter. But once you develop an internal locus of control, self-confidence becomes critical, because the more confident you are in your abilities, the more successful you will be in everything you attempt.

When my daughter Catherine was in sixth grade, she got a bad score on a test. Catherine tried to tell us that she had a bad teacher who didn't like her. Her explanation for bad scores was not lack of study; it was the teacher's fault. I asked her how much she had studied for the test. She said a lot. But when I pinned her down, I found that she had ignored some of her homework. I said she could only tell me about a bad teacher when she did all the work required yet still failed on a test.

It's critical to develop self-confidence in your children early. Don't let them explain their failures as somebody else's fault. Don't allow them to have an external locus of control, never taking responsibility for their results. We want to develop self-confident children who can remember their successes and apply them to the future instead of kids who explain away their failures as somebody else's fault.

In some research, scientists discovered that locus of control led to expectancy shifts. This means that for those with internal locus of control, success would be followed by more success. Those who had an external locus of control would become more pessimistic about the future, as well as more anxious and stressed. Internals tend to attribute outcomes of events to their own control. Therefore they would be much more willing to study harder to achieve a better test score, or practice and work out more to win a game. They would work harder to advance their careers.

The great basketball player Michael Jordan was interviewed by *Sixty Minutes* reporter Steve Kroft. Kroft asked if he always won. Jordan laughed and said, "Not always." Kroft then asked how he coped with loss. Jordan said he keeps playing and practicing until he wins.

This is a good example of how a person with an internal locus of control regards events in his life.

An external person often says, "Why try? It won't work anyway. It's all based on fate, or the influence of powerful people." Sometimes the person believes that the world is too complex for them to successfully control what happens to them.

According to one study, self-confident internals exhibited two critical characteristics: (1) a high achievement orientation and (2) a lower focus on outer circumstances, such as rejection. There are many situations where authors' books were rejected fifty times before they were published. (I know from personal experience what rejection from a publisher is like.) Rejection is tough. During seminars, I say that I was rejected so often in high school that girls I didn't even know would call me on the phone and say, "Don't ask me out."

George Lucas, of *Star Wars* fame, spent four years shopping his first script to various studios and racking up many rejections in the process. He obviously had an internal locus of control, never letting his negative voice get to him. Because of his persistent self-confidence and his dogged determination, *Star Wars* became the highest-grossing movie of all time. He was only paid $200,000 for his first *Star Wars* movie, but he was a very smart negotiator. He accepted the money but negotiated to keep the merchandising rights. The licensing rights to Chewbacca, Han Solo, Luke Skywalker, and other characters made him hundreds of millions of dollars. It wasn't that he was impervious to rejection, but that his internal locus of control made him believe that his ability and ideas would eventually prevail. This is a great example of inner self-confidence.

According to some research, people with an internal locus of control tend to be in better physical shape and have more academic success. They also believe that hard work and focus will help them get better grades, while externals feel they have no control, no matter what they do.

In one study, scientists discovered that excessive gambling behavior is governed by an external focus. Internals are more reserved and cautious, while externals tend to take more risks. How often have you seen a poker player in movies put everything into a pot? A more cautious gambler, on the other hand, folds more quickly.

Many years ago in Laughlin, Nevada, my brother Kevin and I were playing the roulette table. We bet only on black and red, not on numbers. We always played 30 percent odds of winning. If red won, we would put a dollar on black. If black won, we would put a dollar on red. The only thing that gave the bet less than a 50 percent chance of winning was the 00 slot; there was always that chance. I remember that the dealer got so irritated at our gambling caution that she said, "You guys are so boring! I want you to play another table." But at the end of the evening, we got free drinks and were ahead a hundred dollars. This is an example of a cautious internal versus a shoot-for-the-moon external.

There are health benefits to being an internal also. In one study of 7500 British people, scientists found that ten-year-olds who had an internal locus of control were less likely to be overweight at thirty years old. They also tended to have much higher levels of self-esteem and self-confidence.

Self-Efficacy

There's one other aspect of self-confidence. It's called *self-efficacy*. This refers to the belief that you can accomplish an activity. In some studies, people with a high degree of self-efficacy in one area were able to generalize their self-confidence into other areas. For example, someone who is a great golfer tends to have a higher level of self-confidence playing tennis. Someone who is a great student seems to be more confident they can write a work of fiction, even though the two skills may be unrelated. This means self-confidence in one area may be a huge benefit in achieving success in other areas. Or at least your confidence may make you more willing to try.

I played tennis for two years on the international Grand Prix tennis tour from 1976 through 1978. Recently I played with a bunch of my friends in Palm Springs at a weekend tournament. There was a pickleball court at the same country club. Between matches, a bunch of us decided we were going to try the new sport, which is on a miniature tennis court with wooden paddles. None of us had played pickleball before, but because of our tennis ability, all of us were confident we could be good at any racket sport. Of course, none of us were even passably good in the beginning, but because of our self-efficacy in tennis, we competed nearly as ferociously as the pros. It was great fun.

So one way of developing self-confidence in one area is reminding yourself of your expertise in another. This is how self-efficacy helps you generalize self-confidence in other areas. One reason I pushed my three daughters to play sports when they were young was to make them more confident in other areas as adults.

Two

The Magic of Goals

According to Dr. Ivan Joseph, athletic director and soccer coach at Ryerson University, self-confidence is a key component in selecting soccer players for scholarships. Joseph says that parents will approach him and talk about their kids. They will say, "My child has great vision." Or, "My child is able to see the whole field better than any other kids out there. Or, "My child has a left-foot strike better than anybody at his school."

But what Joseph looks for the most is not the students' soccer skill sets but their self-confidence. He looks for students who believe in themselves, never lose sight of their goals, and will strive to win no matter what the odds. He has some very simple yet effective techniques you can use to develop self-confidence.

First, you need repetition. (Author Malcolm Gladwell discusses the 10,000-hour rule. He says, if you do anything for 10,000 hours, you'll become an expert.) Joseph tells the story of a goalie he recruited from South America. While the goalie had good feet, his hands were like stone. No matter what was thrown, he would drop it. So Joseph made the goalie catch 350 soccer balls at the goal net every day for eight months. The goalie with stone hands is now playing pro soccer in Europe at the highest levels.

Most people would also be willing to catch 350 balls, but for only a short period. They won't do something for 10,000 hours. They'll quit when it gets tough. They'll bail out when they get bored. They won't put in the hard yards to get the things they want. J.K. Rowling was rejected thirteen times by publishers before she was able to convince one to publish the Harry Potter series. Because of her great persistence, Rowling became the first billion-dollar author the world had ever seen. As you have undoubtedly heard, Edison tried 10,000 light bulbs before one worked. He was known to say that with each mistake, he narrowed it down one more.

Second, very highly self-confident people have uplifting self-talk. Many of us talk to ourselves negatively. We'll say things like: "I hope I don't mess up again." "I hope I don't make that mistake today." "I can't believe how stupid I am." Self-talk is a little like the baseball pitcher who says to himself, "Don't throw high and inside on this batter." Sure enough, on the next pitch, he throws the ball high and inside, exactly what he did not want to do. The mind has a difficult time filtering negative self-talk from positive self-talk. In other words, if you talk to yourself negatively, negative things happen. If you talk to yourself positively, positive things happen.

When I was in middle of a tennis match many years, ago I double-faulted on a key point. I berated myself and actually said out loud, "What a stupid shot. I have to be the worst tennis player at this club." Sure enough, I lost the match, because I played even worse on the next points as a result of my negative self-talk. That's why athletes have to have amnesia. They have to totally forget their past mistakes, thinking only about the success of the next point.

Third, Joseph mentions that you should get away from anybody who will tear you down. I call this "the theory of the thousand cuts." It's not the elephants that get you, it's the mosquitoes. If one person says you can't do something, maybe you can get over it. But if many people diminish your goals or ability, perhaps you start believing them. Think about the people around you. Do they support your goals and your abilities? Do they uplift you, or do they build themselves up by diminishing you?

Lastly, Joseph mentions self-confidence as an ability to catalog your own past success. I remember my daughter Caroline playing tennis. I watched one of her matches and asked, "How did you do?" She said, "I played great, Dad. I was really on today." Was she playing the same match that I saw? She barely touched the ball. The other team hit to her partner 90 percent of the time. But how Caroline interpreted her playing was everything.

I try to remember how I did the last time. But deeper than that, I tend to remember my mistakes more vividly than my successes. There is a theory among pro athletes that the pain of losing is worse than the joy of winning. Highly self-confident people will remember success more intensely than failure. They will catalog successful situations and try to forget the events in which they did poorly. Or they will reinterpret and recharacterize those past poor performances simply as learning experiences, helping them to become better. If you are a person who best remembers poor performances instead of great ones, this could be difficult. But practice makes perfect. Catch yourself remembering your great successes and reward yourself for them.

Setting Goals

One of the most important paths to a self-confident life is achieving goals. To be confident means that you have already experienced success. The best way of building self-confidence is to steadily achieve your goals. Computer scientist Alan Kay once said, "The best way to predict the future is to invent it." If you know your values, you will have the ability to set goals in accordance with what you believe is important. The conflict and discomfort in reaching those goals will be minimized, because what you're working for is what you really want—your heart's desire.

But how do really successful people set goals, and how do goals work in building your self-confidence? The answer is slicing the big goals down to manageable pieces.

Slicing

Goals may seem pretty intimidating at first. You have big audacious goals, but how you do get started?

How do you eat an elephant? One bite at a time.

The technique of slicing is a big help. There are two ways to use slicing. *Slicing down* is a way to segment major concepts into smaller ones. For example, breaking the category *animal* into smaller sections might mean to slice it down into *marsupials* or *fowl* or *rodents*. Slicing down from the topic of *machine* might be to break the category into a smaller component like *car* or *computer*.

A *slice up* means the reverse: to expand something from a specific category into a broader one. To slice up *car* might mean expanding the concept to *transportation* or *trip*. To slice up *anxiety* might mean to generalize into *psychological discomfort*.

Slicing is important because it helps you organize your goals into a specific plan. I remember when I was in college, I wanted to earn both a PhD and an MD. But I became bogged down in just earning my doctorate. If I had known about slicing, I would have organized my life to earn my PhD within three years; then I would have begun medical school. I would have worked backward, month by month, accomplishing what was needed, in order to accomplish even bigger goals.

You can use slicing to achieve more abstract goals too. While the value of generosity sounds like something rather intangible, a developer named William Lyon made it tangible enough to touch, in the form of the Orangewood Children's Home, in Orange County, California. In fact, Lyon gave more than $250,000 a year to this charity, a refuge for molested and abused children.

Though he may not have thought of it this way, Lyon took his value of generosity and sliced it down to the tangible goal of giving a specific amount of money away. He then sliced his goal down again into the very specific action of giving money to a single charity, the Orangewood Children's Foundation.

Let's suppose that your goal is to work in the beauty industry. If you were to slice that down, it might be parsed into a smaller goal of becoming a beautician. You might slice it down further into enrolling in a two-year cosmetology program in which you'd learn how to design hair and various other beauty secrets.

Years ago, I wanted to become famous. When I was fourteen, I went with a friend to a Herb Alpert concert at the San Diego Sports Arena. In the late 1960s, Alpert's group, the Tijuana Brass, was among the most popular in the nation. When I stepped into the arena, I was shocked to see at least 10,000 fans packed in the seats. As I sat there, I became obsessed with the thought of one day being someone special. I never again wanted to be just an unrecognized face in the crowd. I wanted to walk into a huge group of people and have everyone recognize me.

Many years later, my career of writing books and speaking around the world is likely the outcome of what happened at that sports arena. Your values stay with you and become part of your unconscious, directing much of what you do every day.

This makes sense. Think about all the goals you once wanted to accomplish but didn't have the confidence in yourself to complete. Often you quit because your goals didn't align with your values. They weren't important enough for you, because you didn't believe in them enough.

Years ago I was pushed into playing basketball because of my height. I wanted to make the team but didn't have the motivation to practice as hard as some of the other kids. Predictably, I was cut. Even though I said otherwise, making the team wasn't valuable enough to make the sacrifices necessary to be a good player.

Part of self-confidence is aligning what you want and what you are willing to work for. It's easy to fail attempting things you never wanted to do in the first place. That leads to discouragement, an enemy of self-confidence. Likewise, it's tough to discipline yourself to achieve better grades in college if you never had a desire to get a college degree. It's equally tough to lose weight, no matter how many diet books you read, if you think a slim figure isn't really worth working on. And no matter how many times you tell others that you really want to spend more time with your family, if you don't place sufficient value on doing so, you won't organize your work life to be at home more.

It's very hard to achieve goals that are in direct contrast with your values. Goals are important, but values are their bedrock foundation. If the values underlying your self-confidence are shaky, your goals will be as well.

A recent poll showed that 52 percent of all executives said if they'd known early in their careers that they'd still be in their current jobs, they'd never have started that career in the first place. My lawyer is one of these executives. He really doesn't like to practice law. He would have preferred to go into business as an entrepreneur, but now he's financially committed to raising a family of three boys. How confident do you think he was and will be in trying to spend the hours necessary to build his practice? But if you do something you love, the money will follow.

Four Key Components of Setting Goals

Are you ready to set achievable goals? There are four key points to remember when setting goals. They are:

1. **Be specific.** Think of tangible and specific goals you can work toward, such as "I want to complete my college education in five years" or "I want to be a top-level manager in my current company in five years." A desire to be successful is a common goal, but success is different for everyone. You need to think about what's most important to you. Then slice the goal down into bite-sized pieces. Find specific words and phrases to describe it.

Likewise, use measurable criteria so that you can judge whether or not you've reached your goals. Don't worry if they seem big. There are no unrealistic goals, only unrealistic time frames. It may sound clichéd, but it's better to plan something big and fall short than to set your sights too low.

2. **Schedule for short-, medium-, and long-term goals.**
The short term means in the near future. The medium term is the
next three to five years. The long term is more than five years away.

Develop a long-term plan. Then set medium- and short-term
goals to get there. When I consulted in the late 1970s with the New
York Life Insurance Company, I asked a salesman for one goal that
would motivate him. He said, "To be happy." I told him to write
down three specific achievements that would contribute to his sense
of happiness. He came up with a 560SEL Mercedes and $100,000 in
liquid investments. He also wanted to be home at 5:00 p.m. daily so
he could play with his kids.

3. **Be willing to sacrifice to achieve your objectives.** If
your goal is to read a book each week, you're going to have to make
the time to do it. This might mean watching less TV, taking public
transportation, or sleeping less at night. Can you do this? Are you
willing to do this?

My bother Kevin markets our training videos to small and
medium-sized businesses. He is a brilliant leader, often coaxing stel-
lar performance out of mediocre people. One salesperson, Robert,
was on his way to making more money than he had ever dreamed
of. The problem was that Robert would go out on drinking and drug
binges for days at a time. Kevin gave him warnings that he ignored,
and finally Kevin fired him. For two weeks, Robert begged for his
job back. Kevin felt sorry for the young guy and hired him again.
But he also let Robert know that if this behavior occurred again, he
would be gone.

Within one month, Robert again engaged in drinking and
drugs. He didn't come to work for three days. Kevin asked him why
he was willing to give up a job he said he so desperately wanted.

Robert admitted that he didn't have the self-confidence to say no to his friends when they wanted to go out. He also admitted he didn't have the confidence to stay sober in the long term. Robert wasn't willing to defer rejection from his friends now for a greater pleasure later. And because of his low self-esteem, he was vulnerable to the influence of bad friends.

4. **Maintain self-confidence in your quest to achieve what you want.** As Henry Ford said, "Obstacles are those frightful things you see when you take your eyes off your goal." Without the confidence in your ability to put dreams together, you only have aspirations that never become reality.

One way to maintain confidence in yourself is to carry representations of your goals with you. For example, when I played pro tennis, one player I knew confided that he carried a photo of the U.S. Open trophy in his wallet. Every morning he would take it out and stare at it during breakfast. It helped him stay motivated for the rest of the day.

You might set aside a few minutes every day to review pictures of your goals in order to keep them constantly in mind. In this way you can take stock of your progress and make corrections to ensure that you're on target.

Concentrating on Outcomes

If a *goal* can be defined as an objective you wish to achieve by a certain date, an *outcome* is a goal you experience before you achieve it. I once heard the difference between goals and outcomes defined by one of my mentors, Jeannie LaBorde, this way: Goals and objectives are like pencils in a box that has been newly opened. Outcomes, on the other hand, are the same pencils, sharpened and well used.

Here is a five-step approach to creating outcomes for yourself.

1. Focus on a tangible outcome. Remember that outcomes are goals you can actually see, hear, and feel. While owning a new house is a goal, seeing that house with vaulted ceilings, a cherry-wood kitchen, and a veranda overlooking the ocean is an outcome.

2. Be positive in how you plan for your outcomes.

3. Sense and perceive the way you will feel when you achieve your outcomes.

4. Make sure they fit neatly with the outcomes of those who are important to you.

5. Make sure your outcomes incorporate short-, medium-, and long-term goals.

Let's look more closely at step 1. For example, if your goal is to become rich, your outcome would be to specify the amount of money that will make you wealthy. More specifically, if the goal is to make a six-figure income, the desired outcome might be to make an annual salary of $101,500. You also need to visualize and experience what it will be like earning more than $100,000.

If your goal is to have a better family life, your outcome might be to imagine yourself spending at least an hour per day talking or interacting with your wife and kids.

If your goal is to become more educated, the outcome might be to achieve an MBA within three years. You would imagine what it would be like in the executive suite of a large company.

The second step in achieving outcomes is to be positive about the things you want. I heard one divorced parent say, "My goal is to make sure I keep my ex-husband from getting custody of my child." This isn't an ideal outcome, because this person may end up causing grief not only for herself but for her child. A more positive outcome would be, "My goal is to make sure my child has a consistent and stable home life." Positive outcomes are easier to achieve and avoid conflict with other aspects of your life.

Another kind of positive outcome occurs when you work toward something that other people believe in. Take smoking as an example. Not only will other people be able to relate to your goal of quitting, they can encourage and help you stay confident as you work toward it.

The third step is to perceive how you will feel when you have achieved your outcomes. Researchers in language, neuroprocessing, and psycholinguistics have discovered that people primarily think using one of three senses: sight, sound, and feeling. It's easy to apply this information to step 3.

For example, if your goal is to be wealthy and your desired outcome is to make $100,000 next year, you might visualize $100,000 in neat, new green dollar bills in a paper bag stamped by the U.S. Treasury. Or as you flip your fingers through these bills, you might hear the sound cards make, as you shuffle them in a deck. Or you might feel the slightly rough edges on these bills and note that the paper feels a bit more porous than the writing paper you find in your notebook or textbook. In this way, you're able to see, hear, or feel what a desired outcome is like before you actually achieve it.

You can't do this with goals. Goals are simply things you'd like to accomplish, while outcomes give you a way to actually experience the goal before you strive to achieve it.

The fourth step in achieving outcomes is to make sure your desires dovetail with the values of others in your life. I recently met a woman who wanted to spend money fixing up her house. Her husband's goal was to move into a new house. He didn't want to spend any more money on their existing home, so his wife's refurbishing goal was in direct conflict with his. If she had asked her husband more about his own desired outcomes, she might have discovered that he was interested in increasing the value of their home for later resale. If she had presented the refurbishing idea as a way to build resale value, they might have been able to dovetail their outcomes together.

The fifth step in achieving outcomes is to create short-, medium-, and long-term goals and objectives. Let's use smoking again as an example. Suppose you want to stop smoking in three months. You might schedule a checkpoint for next week for three fewer cigarettes per day. You might also set a goal of how many cigarettes you will be smoking at the end of two months.

When sculptor Auguste Rodin was asked how he created his remarkable statues, he responded, "I choose a block of marble and chop off whatever I don't need." This might be a good approach. Whatever you do, don't copy the techniques used by the various law-enforcement agencies in the following joke:

The LAPD, the FBI, and the CIA were all trying to prove that they were the best at apprehending criminals. The president of the United States decided to give them a test. He released a rabbit into a forest, and each organization was assigned to catch it.

The CIA went in. They placed animal informants throughout the forest. They questioned all plant and mineral witnesses. After three months of extensive investigations, they concluded that rabbits did not exist.

The FBI went in. After two weeks with no leads, they burned the forest, killing everything in it, including the rabbit, and they made no apologies. The rabbit had it coming.

The LAPD went in. They came out two hours later with a badly beaten bear. The bear was yelling, "OK! OK! I'm a rabbit! I'm a rabbit!"

A couple of years ago I met a stressed mom who complained about all the work she had to do and the lack of time to do it in. She knew what she didn't want out of life but couldn't seem to think of what she did want. I asked her what she valued, and of course she said her kids. I asked what her goals were for them, and she had a list of things she wanted: for them to have a good education, to be happy at home, to feel protected, and to feel loved all the time.

I asked her to tell me how she would know if her kids were getting a good education. She said they would be on the honor roll at school. I then asked her how she could ensure that they made the honor roll. She said if they diligently completed their homework every day, they would make it.

Puzzled, I asked her how that would help her feel less stressed. She said that most of her stress was with the kids after school. They fought and messed the house up while she was making dinner. I asked, "If they did their homework every day before watching TV, kept out of your way while you were making dinner, and didn't fight, would you feel less stressed?"

She smiled and said, "If you can do that, I'll be your friend for life."

I went one step further. I asked her to think about what her dream house would look and sound like at the end of the workday. She said, "It's all quiet. My kids are studying in their rooms. They pop in once in a while to ask me a homework question, say 'Thanks, Mom,' and go back to their work. I hear them talking to each other without bickering. I then ask them to come to dinner, and they both tell me their homework is done." The woman was surprisingly detailed in her mind of what a blissful household looked, sounded, and felt like.

Uncovering this overworked mom's values and goals was the first step towards creating the outcomes she wanted in her life. While a lot of work remained, she was now on the right track to do it—and in fact *did* do it.

Like this woman, you too can assess your values, set goals, and concentrate on outcomes to achieve the self-confidence necessary to make them come to life. This may be the stuff dreams are made of, but dreams can—with self-confidence—come true.

Three

Using Self-Confidence to Stop Anxiety

A nxiety and stress are enemies of self-confidence. Much of this comes from change, which as you learned before, creates stress, and is followed by avoidance behavior.

Another enemy of self-confidence is performance anxiety. Whether you are an actor, musician, or athlete, or are even giving a business presentation, you need self-confidence, and lots of it. I'm sure you've heard a speaker with low self-confidence giving excuses that they are not very prepared or haven't given a speech before. Or a speaker with high self-confidence getting the group involved with lots of participation and humor.

I spoke in Las Vegas recently when the speaker who followed me actually spoke on presentation skills. He said the number-one fear in human beings is speaking in front of a group. The number-two fear is dying. The number-three fear is presumably dying while speaking in front of a group. I laughed but thought that is amazingly true.

Think of the things you could do and what a career builder it would be if you had the self-confidence to speak in front of any group on a topic you felt passionate about.

Another aspect of becoming self-confident is to overcome the fears that destroy it. These are irrevocably intertwined with the expectation of pain and are the opposite of living a self-confident life. As I mentioned earlier, there are four fears that nearly all of us feel in our lives and that sabotage our self-esteem: the fear of rejection, the fear of looking foolish, the fear of failure, and the fear of success.

I jokingly say that we are born with only three fears: the fear of falling, the fear of loud noises, and the fear of the IRS. Many of these other fears were given to you by your parents, and the way you were brought up indicates the degree to which you have them. One of my mentors in the 1980s was a famous life-insurance sales guru named John Savage. He had eight kids. He used to say during seminars that he had a sign in his basement that read, "Notice to the children. It's either my way or the highway." The sign below that read, "This family can get by with seven kids." But he was a wonderful father and constantly focused his children on their abilities and gifts instead of their failures, helping them become self-confident in anything they wanted to do.

The reality is these fears are all irrational. There's a difference between irrational and rational fears. If you are a salesperson who asks a prospect for business and gets the response, "Get out and stay out!" you would feel an irrational fear of rejection. But if that same prospect reached for an ax and said, "Get out!" you would feel a very rational fear of rejection, and thank goodness you have that.

I experienced irrational fear when I began my speaking career. After finishing graduate school, I wanted to stay in applied psychology in some way, yet the academic teaching competition was stiff, and fellowships were few and far between. Nor did I relish working in academia any longer. So I started to speak to associations and professional groups as a way of advertising my consulting skills. Unfortunately, I was too young to be taken credibly, and I was rarely asked to consult. But I was flooded with speaking requests. I guess they thought I could do less damage speaking than through extensive consulting engagements.

The problem was, I was so terrified of speaking in front of groups that I was unable to sleep a wink before a speech for two years. To this day, I feel my biggest achievement has been overcoming that fear.

During my seminars I jokingly explained this difference between rational and irrational fears through an experience at an airport. I was at the ticket counter in Denver, waiting to board a flight. The gate agent asked me where I wanted to sit. I looked out the window of the terminal and saw the airplane was a DC-10. This was a crash-and-burn, turning-cartwheels-in-Iowa-cornfields DC-10. A DC-10 had just crashed about a month earlier, and I felt a little nervous. The gate agent said, "There are people waiting behind you. Where would you like to sit?" I looked at her and said," I want to sit in the safest place in that airplane. I want to sit in the black box." What is that thing made out of, and why don't they make airplanes out of the same material? (The black box isn't even black, it's orange.)

First, the fear of rejection is a self-confidence killer. We did a study among 1000 financial salespeople and discovered that fear of rejection nearly ended their careers. It was the single biggest reason for failure in financial-service sales. Ninety-five percent of the people surveyed said it was their single biggest fear in their business. (I jokingly say that the other 5 percent lied.) One Boston producer told me he makes his secretary call clients and prospects for appointments. I said, "Don't you think that you would be more successful making those phone calls." He said, "Of course. But I don't want to get rejected."

The second fear that debilitates self-confidence is the fear of looking foolish. Do you feel a desire to appear smart and savvy among everybody you meet? This is more than wanting to make a good first impression; it's your desire to have everybody think well of you.

Here's a test. If someone you don't know well uses a word you also don't know, would you be willing to ask them what it means? Because if you do, you could risk looking stupid. I make a point of always asking what new words are, no matter whom I talk to. Sometimes even the person using the word doesn't know what it means.

There have been two situations in my life that were completely embarrassing. I could look back and be traumatized, with shattered self-esteem, linking my self-confidence to these embarrassing failures, or I could find humor in the situations, realizing an internal locus of control and knowing that I have power over events.

A few years ago, as I was in a restroom washing my hands, a guy in the stall next to me said loudly, "What's up?" I didn't have any idea who it was, and said, "I'm fine. How are you?" No response. Ten seconds later, the same man said, "What's happening?" I still didn't know who this was but didn't want to be rude and said, "Nothing. Just working today." Just then the guy in the stall said, "Hang on for second. There's some idiot in here trying to talk to me." He was on a cell phone the whole time. Totally embarrassed, I was out of the bathroom in two seconds.

The second situation in my life was even more embarrassing. I actually tell the story now during seminars just to get laughs. In

1985, I spoke to a big group in Hong Kong. While there, I bought three new tailored suits. Back in those days not only were the suits of wonderful quality (or so I thought), but they were really cheap. I was a young guy and didn't really know the difference until the next week when I spoke in Seattle. Thirty minutes into my speech in front of 600 attendees, a guy in the front row held up a sheet of paper with the words "Your fly is down." Now I'm used to getting heckled as a speaker; in fact, I really love audience participation. But I thought this was rude and over the top. I just ignored him when he started pointing at his rude sheet of paper. I decided to humor him and silently mouthed the word "Really?" He nodded. I turned away from the crowd during my speech, and sure enough my fly was down. But it gets worse. As I tried to zip up, I realized that the Hong Kong tailor had put in a plastic zipper. It wouldn't zip up. By this time all 600 attendees knew what was happening and laughed. I took my jacket off and tied it around my waist. I laughed and said, "A speaker's worst fears have just been realized." The whole group laughed again, and I went on with my speech.

I know a lot of people who would never have given a speech again after this trauma. But while I was embarrassed at the moment, I laughed later. Now it makes for a very funny story.

This is what self-confidence boils down to. Can you take an embarrassing, sometimes debilitating situation, and make it work for you? Your fear of looking foolish will fight you. But your self-confidence will be able to overcome it.

The next enemy of self-confidence is fear of failure. Will you work harder to keep from losing than you will to win? Will you work harder to keep what you have than to get something better? People with a fear of failure say, "If it's not broken, don't fix it." People without a fear of failure say, "You don't have to be sick to get better."

One aspect of fear of failure has to do with security. People with this fear look at money as security, not as a resource or a tool. Most decamillionaires—those with more than $10 million in net worth—have been through bankruptcy or multiple business failures before making their millions. The common thread among them is their willingness to take risks. As they do, they become more confident with incremental success. That builds a higher desire to take more risk to become more successful.

Are you that way now? Is your self-confidence so high that you could go through bankruptcy or failure knowing that it wouldn't be the end? That's what self-confidence does. And that's what you can build today.

Living a self-confident life does not mean living without failure. Even the most confident people alive face challenges and pitfalls, but they know how to triumph over them, or at least to rise above them.

Often misfortune can be a great teacher. When you fail, you learn volumes about what you do well and what you need to work on. Your strengths and abilities as well as your weaknesses are put in proper perspective. Interestingly, some researchers believe that those who don't fail enough are actually sleeping their way through life, taking too few risks, while those who fail and learn from their losses are usually the ones who are most likely to succeed later.

A salesperson I knew feared she would be unable to complete an advanced sales course. The program would have helped her increase her ability to sell to prospects in more affluent markets, but she felt that if she failed to complete it successfully, she wouldn't be able to handle the rejection from her associates. She already doubted her abilities and wasn't willing to risk her self-confidence further if she didn't complete the course.

Predictably, her avoidance behavior prevented her from advancing her sales ability and production. She admitted later that if she'd done the training, she would have increased her income by $100,000 per year.

Eliminate *Failure* from Your Vocabulary

One way to dissipate your fear of failure is deleting the word from your vocabulary altogether. Don't say the word *failure*, think it, or listen to others who say it. See only results from what you do, some of them positive, some of them negative, all of them educational. Top business people don't use the word. Instead they use words like *setback*, *correction*, or *modification*.

Force Yourself to Fail

You might also consider the novel idea of *forcing* yourself to fail in order to realize once and for all that it's not fatal. Some colleges actually offer courses in failure, assigning projects that are guaranteed to go wrong so that people can learn to desensitize themselves to emotional paralysis when failure happens in the real world.

There are gender differences with failure as well. Women tend to experience failure differently than men. They also tend to avoid failure to a greater extent than males. So it's even more critical for women to recognize this and challenge themselves with small but frequent chances of failure. This could be competing in sports, games, or projects. Through sports, boys often learn that failure is never fatal. But unless you challenge yourself with small failures now, you will not allow yourself to risk greater failure later.

Some research has shown that firstborns in a family have a greater fear of failure than other siblings, because much more parental expectation is put on them than others. Some recent research has shown in larger families lastborns have the same level of expectation. I jokingly say that parents realize they messed up on the first few kids, so now's your chance for pressure.

I was the firstborn among four kids. My mom told me that she knew there was pressure on me when my father put an ad in the *Portland Oregonian* newspaper announcing the birth of their son, Dr. Kerry Johnson.

Don't tell my life-insurance company, but I heli-ski in Canada, jumping out of helicopters in the Powder Mountains of British Columbia. I have been twice and will soon go again. But it is very dangerous. When I was there a few years ago, three skiers died in an avalanche. I remember the first briefing at the dinner the night before the first ski day. There were 100 skiers watching videos of avalanches overcoming skiers. One guide mentioned that every skier would wear a transponder so that others in the group could locate him, but there was only a five-minute window before the skier died. I started thinking that I could cup my hands over my face, creating an air pocket. I thought I could last perhaps a few hours in the snow. I stood up in the group, raised my hand, and asked, "Why five minutes?" The guide said, "If you get caught in an avalanche, the branches, rocks, and debris will rip limbs off, causing the skier to bleed to death in five minutes."

That really grabs your attention. I don't think I slept a wink that night wondering what would happen the next day. In fact the guides are so professional that they test the snow gliding layers on every other run, and can read the ski areas like a book. But fear of failure in heli-skiing can be very, as we said before, rational.

The last of the fears that sabotage self-confidence is the fear of success. This is the most common as well as the most confusing fear. Everybody wants success, correct? We'd all do well to remember Oscar Wilde's famous quote: "There are only two tragedies in life: one is not getting what one wants, and the other is getting it."

To use a benign example, say you're on the tee of the eighteenth hole, and are the last one to drive. If you can just maintain your lead, you can have bragging rights until the next outing. You position yourself over the ball, lining up your head and feet perfectly, draw your club back, and follow through, staring down the fairway. But instead of seeing your ball in flight, you hear the laughter of your friends behind your back because you've totally missed the ball. Whoops. Fear of success strikes again.

Yet many of us achieve success and stop ourselves. When this happens, failure occurs. The memory of failure debilitates your confidence. Have you ever experienced complacency? Or has your business been on a plateau? Has any other area of your life plateaued? This could be fear of success. In the book *The Impostor Phenomenon*, the author points out that many very successful people feel they don't deserve the success they experience. They feel they have been lucky, but someone eventually may discover they are not that good. This low self-esteem and low level of self-confidence can cause even successful people to feel anxiety and dread.

In 1986 tennis player Carling Bassett was in the finals of a televised tournament in Amelia Island, Florida. She was ahead of Chris Evert, the reigning champion. Bassett won the first set 6–1 and was ahead in the second set 5–0 serving to end the match. She double-faulted the first point. She netted a backhand on the second point and soon lost the game. Evert went on to win the next six straight games as well as the third set, 6–0. Bassett was asked afterwards how she could have lost that match. She said candidly, "Who Chris Evert was mattered more than how she played." Bassett could not see herself beating Chris Evert and winning the match. This is a good example of fear of success.

Fear of success is not limited just to tennis or sports. It could be any area of your life. When I was a stockbroker in 1981, we learned how stocks grew within predictable patterns called *resistance* and *support levels*. A support would be a stock's low trading range, and resistance would be a stock's upper trading range. We learned that once a stock traded below a support level, it was a good time to buy. When a stock traded above a resistance level, it was a good time to sell.

Your life and your career may closely parallel how stocks trade. When you hit an income level, for example, $200,000 a year, you may stop yourself from making more money. But when your income reaches a support level of $40,000 a year, you may work eighteen hours a day to increase it.

At the start of my consulting career in 1981 with New York Life, one new salesperson made $25,000 a year as a schoolteacher. In her first six months selling life insurance, she made $20,000. Guess how much she made in her next six months? You guessed it—$5000. She was so adapted to her $25,000 income as a schoolteacher that she sabotaged her chances to make more. That is fear of success.

A salesman recently told me that he seemed to be limiting himself to making about $40,000 a year. When I asked why he wasn't growing in his career, he mentioned that his father was a teacher with a master's degree who only made $25,000 a year. This salesperson had only a high-school graduation certificate. He felt so guilty about making more money than his father that he put off building his career and sabotaged his income.

Progressive Collapse

Right now you should be asking, "How do you rid yourself of these four fears?" The answer is that you've spent decades of your life developing them. It will take you at least that long to get over them. Isn't that encouraging? You will never be able to eradicate them. But there is a wonderful way to cope. One is called *rational emotive therapy*, based on the work of the pioneering psychotherapist Albert Ellis. He called it the *ABC technique*: antecedent, behavior, consequences. I call this technique *progressive collapse*. You are actually collapsing the symptoms of fear into irrational and illogical caricatures you can easily deal with.

Surprisingly simple, the technique merely discusses what the triggering event is, what your response to it is, and the consequence of the behavior. For example, you have never given a speech before, although you are an expert in your field. The biggest group you've given a speech to is to four or five colleagues over a glass of wine. But an association would like you to speak to 500. It's a great career-building opportunity, and you are absolutely terrified. You can't say no, because you couldn't live with yourself for not taking advantage of this chance to advance your career. But if you say yes, you might not be well-received, and you could be embarrassed or even seen as a failure. That could even retard your chances of moving up in your company. To make matters worse, your self-confidence is very low because you had a panic attack giving a speech in college.

Ellis's ABC technique would ask you to evaluate the antecedent. What created the stress response for you? Was it the invitation, or your self-sabotaging memory of failure in college? What is the behavior? Stress anxiety, possibly an avoidance-behavior desire to say no to the invitation?

But then there are the consequence. This is where it really gets good. This process takes you from rational consequences to the ridiculous. For example, instead of saying the speech will go well, you move from a level of low self-confidence and external locus of control and you entertain the notion of a bad speech. But then the ABC technique would ask you for a realistic consequence of giving a bad speech. You could not be thought of as a brilliant expert. What would happen then? It may take you longer to achieve a position that you really want. What would happen then? You may have to publish more. What would happen then? You may have to practice your speaking skills. What would happen then?

Another example: If you are overweight and finally enroll in a diet program yet also decide it would be difficult to risk failure, you'd think of all the bad things that could happen. You would first say to yourself, "If I don't lose the weight, I'll feel upset."

You'd then hear a voice inside your head say, "What then?"

"Well, then, I'll be depressed," you'd answer.

The voice would ask, "What then?"

"Then I'll probably be irritated with myself," you'd respond.

"What then?"

"I'll probably eat more," you'd answer.

"What then?"

"I guess I'll eventually try another weight-loss program."

By carrying this process to an extreme, you're suddenly faced with the reality that the worst than can happen isn't all that bad. It's not as frightening as you thought. Progressive collapse forces you to take a realistic look at the worst that could happen rather than to indulge in a nightmarish illusion that becomes real because it's never challenged.

As you can see, the consequence of nearly every fear you face ends up being ridiculous. A mentor once told me that success is never forever, and failure is never fatal. It's not just facing fear that's important, it's playing those fears out to the end and realizing that the rationally likely outcomes are not all that devastating. That is what gives you the power to be self-confident in any new thing that you do. It allows you to get past the risk of failure to accomplish things that only risk will provide.

Business owners with ultrahigh net worth are willing to risk failure and bankruptcy because they have been through it already. While it was not pleasant, they end up confident they can get through it.

That's what the ABC technique does for you. It gets you to experience the rational consequences and outcome of any fear, and in the process builds self-confidence so that you can be successful no matter what happens.

Often my clients will ask me if there's a faster way to decrease the stress that comes from psychological fears. One idea is to try some vitamin supplements. Obviously, talk to your doctor before trying any supplements, drugs, or changes to your diet. But there are several vitamins that may serve to calm your jangled nerves and to help the psychological fears pack less punch. One is inositol. This is a L-tryptophan derivative, and works much the same way as turkey does on Thanksgiving. For many people, it has a relaxing effect that lasts for a couple of hours. Many of my clients take between 1000 and 2000 milligrams right before experiencing a stressful situation, like speaking in front of a group or making sales calls.

Another supplement that seems to work effectively is GABA. This comes in 750-milligram tablets. Many people take 1500 milligrams to decrease their anxiety while staying mentally sharp.

When you have any of the fears, it's important to use the techniques I have discussed to eradicate them in the long term. But in the short term perhaps these vitamin supplements can help you maintain calm.

Your doctor can prescribe many other drugs that may work well. Yet most synthetic drugs have side effects. For example, 30 percent of stage performers experience severe stage fright. Even veterans cope with bouts of stage fright every once in a while. Symptoms of stage fright, or panic attacks, are elevated heart rate, shortness of breath, memory loss, and severe perspiration. Many psychiatrists will prescribe propranolol. This is a beta blocker and decreases the heart rate. Beta blockers serve as a barrier against elevated heart rate and reduce these other symptoms. Again whether you use a vitamin supplement, or a synthetic drug, is a decision to be made between you and your doctor.

Diminished Intensity

Another technique, called *diminished intensity*, works well to decrease the power of irrational fears, including the fear of success. To use it, identify how the fear is represented in your mind, then change it.

For example, a salesman recently told me that he doesn't like face-to-face prospecting with professional businesspeople because he feels an intense fear of rejection. It's so debilitating that he freezes up when he's in front of high-income prospects.

I taught him to picture himself seated alone in a movie theater and see himself acting out the troubling experience on the screen. After he watched the experience unfold, he was to play it backwards as if he were rewinding a video player. Then he was to play it forwards, but this time to increase the speed of the movie and put his favorite music to it. When he got to the end, he was again to play it backwards, making it seem like a comical slapstick routine. The experience worked to desensitize him to the panic he normally felt.

Interrupt Your Fear

Simply interrupting your fear while you're in the middle of it can be effective too. For example, think of the last time you felt rejected by someone. It could have been a pretty woman you wanted to ask out, or maybe your boss turned down your request for a raise, or maybe your husband failed to compliment the new bathing suit you spent three hours picking out. Remember the anxiety you felt. Now immediately stand up and walk around for a moment.

Anxiety takes a lot of concentration to maintain. If you can't be attentive, your fear goes away. So if you feel one of your fear patterns is interfering with the confidence you need to control your emotions, do something to interrupt it.

My wife, Merita, became a flight attendant even though she had a fear of heights. When a job with AirCal (which became American Airlines through a merger) came up, she saw the way out of her dead-end bank job. Instead of focusing on the panic she would feel for the first few flights, she concentrated on the glamour of traveling to far-off places she might otherwise never have had the chance to see.

While controlling anxiety can be difficult, psychological researcher Rollo May believes that some anxiety can actually be good. The problem is, there is a very thin line between the anxiety that paralyzes and the kind that helps you win.

The late golfer Payne Stewart won the U.S. Open in 1999 with a twenty-foot putt on the last hole. Phil Mickelson, his closest competitor, had been making amazing putts the whole day, except on the seventeenth hole, where he missed an easy five-footer. If not for that missed putt, Mickelson could have forced a play-off with Stewart and possibly won his first major tournament.

A reporter asked Mickelson if he felt the pressure on the last few holes. He said yes. When asked the same question, Stewart said that he felt anxiety but that he was able to control it.

Controlling anxiety. Maintaining your self-confidence. That's what it's all about.

Staying Self-Confident: The Final Word

A manager recently told me that if he could just motivate his salespeople, profits would skyrocket.

We have to realize that everyone is motivated, whether it's to sit at home in the evenings watching sitcoms or to shop every day of the week or to work on a myriad of other projects or objectives. Being motivated is not the issue. Restructuring objectives and understanding how we handle our perceptions of pleasure and pain are what motivation—or self-confidence—is all about.

Nutritionists say that the average overweight person goes on 1.5 diets annually and tries more than fifteen times to lose weight between the ages of twenty-one and fifty. Predictably, most diets fail.

Stanford researchers also report that most overweight people do not seek professional help, and those who do often drop out of their regimens without losing much weight. The reason is simple: they are unable to continue the dieting program because of the pain involved in trying to stay on a plan, especially if the plan has previously failed for them.

These same researchers have added a new twist to an already sad story: Surveying a ten-year period of medical treatment for obesity, they calculated the percentage of patients who lost significant amounts of weight and found that no more than 25 percent lost as much as twenty pounds and no more than 5 percent lost as much as forty pounds. They also said that those who lost the weight often gained most of it back within a short period of time.

The reason, again, is the pain of staying committed. Losing weight is tough for most people, but it does not have to be. The answer to losing weight lies in the confidence that you can complete a diet successfully and in learning to change the way you perceive the pain and pleasure of dieting. The answer to all such problems lies in understanding the power of mental toughness and the pleasure/pain principle or, in other words, the psychology of self-confidence.

Putting Self-Confidence to Work

1. Think about how you respond to stressful situations. What is your attitude? In short, do you have mental toughness? Use the technique of pattern interrupt to help yourself use positive self-talk.

2. To begin confronting your natural tendency to avoid pain, change the order in which you deal with life's demands. For example, try eating the food you like least first at breakfast, lunch, and dinner. When you get to work tomorrow morning, try doing the most distasteful job first. This should be an activity, like filing, that you've been postponing because it's uncomfortable or just plain isn't fun.

3. Take a few moments and write down three things you know you should do but haven't. This could be anything from prun-

ing trees to doing a performance review to challenging your habit of swearing. Next to these items, write down the expectation of discomfort and pain that's contributing to your procrastination.

Now jot down the pleasure you'll receive as a result of completing these tasks. This could be a financial reward, praise, or even a sense of pride from having done something you are proud of.

Then use the three-step process to restructure the pleasure/pain you associate with these tasks. Also use the technique of planning, learning, observing, and engaging to overcome any procrastination.

4. Make a list of your irrational fears and use the techniques explained in this chapter to deal with them. Try the technique of progressive collapse to deal with the fear of failure. Delete the word *failure* from your vocabulary and see what happens.

5. Use the technique of diminished intensity on another fear, as well as the technique of interrupting your fear. Depending on how advanced your fears are, you may even want to consider the benefits of forcing yourself to fail.

Four
Visualization
and Recasting

The 1989 French Open tennis champion was the youngest winner ever. In fact, teenager Michael Chang nearly lost except for an extraordinary level of self-discipline. Part of what may have contributed to his success was the pictures he kept plastered on his bedroom walls for two years before he won the title—pictures of people winning a Grand Slam tournament. Chang not only had internalized this vision, he had also envisioned every point he'd play on the slow red-clay courts of Roland Garros Stadium in Paris.

When he walked onto the court, he felt as if he'd been there before. He was so committed to fulfilling his envisioned destiny that at one point he served underhanded to Ivan Lendl. He was too tired to serve overhanded because of the pain of cramps, but even so he was able to win his serve. His vision of winning ignited the power that made his self-discipline come alive, and he fought off painful cramps to become one of the top ten players in the world.

In his book *Peak Performers,* Dr. Charles Garfield reports that not only do athletes like Michael Chang understand the value of mental rehearsal, they've been doing it since long before psychologists discovered a name for it. Garfield writes that everything from selling to speaking in front of a group to becoming a better golfer can be improved by practicing mental rehearsal, or visualization.

Visualization

One of the best ways to develop a high level of self-confidence is to visualize yourself having it. When children decorate their bedroom walls with pictures and posters of people they admire, whether it's Superman, Wonder Woman, Teenage Mutant Ninja Turtles, or Michael Jordan, they are using visualization. Vivid mental representations can give them the leverage they need to maintain self-direction. We adults can use the same technique to achieve our objectives.

In the sports world, images are what cause athletes to go from amateur to professional. Hall of Fame running back Walter Payton, in his heyday with the Chicago Bears football team, was once asked by a reporter how he was able to explode so quickly out of the backfield. Payton looked surprised at the question and said, "Why should it be so mysterious? I've run that pattern through the defensive line in my mind at least a thousand times. I've run it so often I knew exactly where the scrimmage-line hole would be."

What is it about pictures—that is, visualizations—that's so crucial to living a self-confident life? There are two factors. One is that pictures allow us to focus on exactly what we're working for. Factor two is that it's difficult to make sacrifices and endure pain if we don't have a clear-cut image of what we're trying to achieve.

Diets fall apart so quickly in part because of the dieter's hunger, but it also has a lot to do with the fact that the person on the diet isn't able to endure the discomfort of short-term hunger and exercise. This is because the discomfort causes the dieter to lose sight of what he's working for. If you've set a goal of losing weight, make sure you create a mental image of the way you would like to look. Turn that image into a big, bright, close, and colorful representation in your mind. Reaccess that memory constantly to keep yourself on track.

Without a picture or mental photograph, we live from pleasure to pleasure, from moment to moment. One reason so few people manage to maintain self-confidence in accomplishing great things in life is that they forget to picture images in their minds of what they want to achieve. This lack of direction dooms them at times to lives of emptiness and at other times to lives of quiet hedonism, in which they constantly move from one good feeling to the next. This may not sound terrible until you see a fifty-year-old who has spent his whole life searching for one good feeling after another and who now finds himself in a job and lifestyle he hates.

Develop Your Visual Side

Developing visual images of self-confidence isn't tricky in the least. You can actually bring yourself from low self-confidence to high by using a mental technique called *recasting*. While deceptively simple, it is used by superstars in all areas to reach short- and long-term goals. You may not have heard of him before, but real-estate developer Donald Bren is one of the ten richest people in America. Bren built his first house at age twenty-five with a $10,000 loan. He went on to become the single largest landowner in southern California, one of America's richest real-estate markets.

How did he do it? Bren had a unique vision of the future. In 1983 he purchased prime Southern California real estate. His goal was to develop it in his lifetime. In his office sat a model of each parcel of raw land parcel, with buildings resting on them as if they were already developed.

Bren is past seventy and close to seeing his scale model become life-sized, but he still arrives at work at 7:00 a.m., pays attention to details, and even eats lunch at his desk.

Mental Substitution

To further develop your visual side, try the technique of mental substitution: On a piece of paper write down the sign of a square root and put some numbers in it. Next to it write down an algebraic equation, one that you can remember. Now write down the symbols of multiplication signs, division signs, and other logarithmic or geometric signs. Concentrate on them. Experience the emotion you feel as you look at them. If you're turned off, you're probably accessing the same experience you had in school when you were learning them.

Now take a minute and close your eyes. Think of a wonderful experience you had in the past, something that you were excited and motivated about, something that was enormously fun. (It will be easier for you to access this experience if it happened to you recently.) Now open your eyes and look back at the piece of paper with the mathematical symbols. Then close your eyes, go back, and ponder the picture of the fun experience in your mind. Next go back to looking at the mathematical symbols. Now close your eyes again and return to the fun experience.

Now think of something emotionally very neutral, such as a road sign or a mountain. Then look back again at the equations.

If you discover that your anxiety over these numerical symbols has decreased, you've just shown yourself that mental images can change your emotions.

Observation

Another way to gain more access to your visual side is to practice observing people. Right now, look at the person nearest you. This could be someone driving in a car, someone walking along the street, or someone lying around the pool. Look at that person for no more than three to four seconds. Now look away.

Now verbally try to recall as many specific features about that person's looks as you possibly can. What color is their clothing? What color is their hair? How tall are they? Are they wearing glasses? How thin or fat are they? Are they wearing tennis shoes, high heels, or flats?

This exercise not only helps develop your visual side, it's also extremely useful in helping you develop your visual memory.

Submodality Focus

Another technique for seeing yourself as more self-confident is submodality focus. Submodality focus has to do with the way we experience events. Some of us experience and remember events by what we see. Others remember what they hear more and still others remember events by how they felt. These 3 modalities of seeing, hearing and feeling make up a large part of how we experience the world.

Some people can be positive or negative about what they experience. But if someone remembers elaborate details about an event or experience, they may have a seeing submodality focus.

I once asked a computer executive who was competing directly with IBM and Hewlett Packard how his day had gone. He said, "Wonderful." He then told me about one of his scientists making a key component work more proficiently. As he discussed this, he was extremely excited. I asked him if anything else had happened during the day, and he told me about at least ten or twenty horrible things that had occurred. These included cash-flow problems, staff shortages, and union negotiations. I then asked him what made the scientific benefit so wonderful. As he remembered, I noticed how elaborate he was in his description of the positive event and how little he said about the negative things.

He was using submodality focus. It's a key ingredient in maintaining self-confidence, and top business people employ it regularly to keep themselves positive.

Association/Disassociation

Another visualization technique that will serve you well is called *association/disassociation*. This is a way to separate yourself from negative and limiting experiences that can wreak havoc with your confidence.

Back in the early 1980s, when I first started my consulting business, I met an interesting guy. Like me, Tom was a young entrepreneur in his mid-twenties. He was involved in the manufacture of fashion roller skates, one of the big fads at the time. Despite his enthusiasm, Tom went bankrupt in 1982. He was down but not out.

I recently saw Tom at a financial-planning symposium. He is now a partner in a mutual-fund company. While we had a cup of coffee, he described his distressing experience. He told me that he had been underfinanced and ill-prepared. He hadn't known how to deal with cash-flow problems or employees.

Tom described this experience in the third person: "Tom had a tough time. The man who loaned Tom money didn't agree with the way Tom was running his business. Unfortunately, Tom got sick and tired of dealing with this person. He and Tom had a parting of the ways."

It was incredible to hear someone talk about himself this way. I don't tell someone a story and refer to myself as "Kerry"; I use *I*. But disassociation was Tom's way of separating himself from the negative experience. It was almost as if he was watching a movie or a television show of himself having a bad experience.

On the other hand, as he told me about his current success, he used the word *I* constantly, as in "*I'm* successful now," "*I'm* making a six-figure income," "*I'm* now a partner with a large financial firm with the best products in the industry." Tom truly was successful.

It should make sense to all of us that the more we relive events in our lives, the greater effect they'll have over our current and future emotions. If we vividly remember successful experiences and deliberately distance ourselves from bad ones, we'll be encouraged—and much more motivated—to risk and try again.

Attachment

One offspring of the association/disassociation technique is called *attachment*, which comes from the concept of psychological conditioning. Attachment is a way of changing negative experiences into positive ones.

Have you ever run into a stranger who wore the same fragrance as that of a loved one? It might be the scent of your mother, wife, husband, or lover. When you got a whiff of it, you instantly thought of that person and possibly of an experience with them.

This can happen with songs, colors, touch—lots of things—and you can put it to work for you. Recall a wonderful experience, a time when you did something great with family or friends. Access that experience right now. For the time being, make it extremely bright, colorful, and close. If you can hear the laughter and feel the smile on your face, so much the better. At the moment when you feel the highest level of enjoyment, touch yourself on your arm or hip or some easily accessible place. Then go back and relive the wonderful experience again, several more times.

This is a stimulus-response technique, similar to the way Pavlov's dog salivate in response to a bell. Stimulus-response is one of the most powerful reactions known in modern psychology. It's also one of the simplest techniques to use. Whenever you feel yourself becoming stressed, touch yourself in the same place. If you've successfully attached the positive experience to that touch, you'll be amazed at what happens.

Likewise, use attachment when you want to mentally plan for success. First, breathe deeply until you relax. Let your mind wander, not concentrating on any one thing. Then start imagining what it is you want to achieve, such as giving a great speech or closing the biggest sale of your life. As you think of this success, touch yourself in the programmed place. Do this a few times and notice the visualization of the great success come back simply by touching yourself. This is almost like a switch turning on a light, but in this case the light is an image that is full of success and power for you.

A key to making mental rehearsal work is to make the experience as real as possible and to use as many senses as you can think of. What does a win taste like? What does it sound, feel, smell, or look like?

Golfer Phil Mickelson won the 1996 Phoenix Open with an incredible, once-in-a-lifetime shot. He was behind a tree on the thirteenth hole and had to make par to stay in the running. Fat chance. A great shot from that position might get him back on the fairway, saving a bogey, but little else. He looked at the green and tried to remember what it had felt like the last time he'd hit an extreme draw from behind a tree.

A draw in golf is virtually a controlled hook, yet the word *control* is generous. This is one of the hardest shots in golf to hit, let alone land in the same fairway you are aiming for. Mickelson lined up the draw and, to the gallery's amazement, curved the banana-shaped shot an astonishing 130 yards onto the green with a pitching wedge. The crowd went wild. When Mickelson was asked by a reporter how he was able to hit such a difficult pitch, he said that he didn't do anything special. He simply remembered what it had felt like the last time he'd hit a draw from behind a tree.

When you remember a successful situation, it is likely in a different mode than the way you remember anxiety or failure. One mortgage-loan broker mentioned that he remembers his best sale as a mental image and experiences sales anxiety as a voice in his mind. When I told him to *see* the next appointment instead of *hear* it, his anxiety and worry disappeared.

Like most motivational philosophers, Saul Miller believes that if you *see* yourself winning, you will be that much closer to doing it. If you *see* yourself doing it, you can improve your sales, management, sports, or any other performance.

In fact, you can experience future success mentally right now. Picture yourself not losing your temper with your three-year-old when he steals a toy from the baby. Instead see yourself calmly, rationally, and effectively handling the situation. Or see yourself drinking a diet shake for breakfast and lunch instead of a hamburger. You might even visualize yourself craving a hamburger but then possessing the confidence to avoid the temptation and drinking that diet shake instead.

Recasting

In addition to using visualization, you can experience future success mentally by recasting your perception of what self-confidence is. Recasting works much like a frame around a picture. A poor frame can make any painting worse, just as a beautiful frame can make even a mediocre painting look substantially better. In some cases, the frame can look better than the picture itself. Recasting is built on the concept that there are no good or bad events in your life; there's only your perception of these events.

Recasting is not exactly visualization. It is more a restructuring of how you think about a concept or idea. For example, if you decide to go into work at 7:00 a.m., your first inclination might be to think, "I will feel tired." To recast that idea might be to think, "If I go into work at 7:00 a.m., I will be able to get an extra two hours of work done without interruption. This in turn will help me to achieve my goals more effectively."

I once developed a friendship with an airline pilot. His emotional picture frame was his career. He connected everything he thought of to flying or something related to it. If he saw a news report about Paris, he'd talk about a recent trip there. If we discussed food, he'd bring up airline cuisine.

Most people don't structure their thoughts to that extent, but we all see life in a way that either limits or empowers us. While my friend was limited in his frame, it certainly served his objective of being a successful pilot. The way he framed the world made even the drudgery of his work enjoyable because he saw the entire world as if it were made for flying.

You can use this concept of recasting in developing self-confidence. The key to recasting is to associate positive experiences with your goals and objectives and to disregard the factors in these experiences that seem to be obstacles, or at least to see them as opportunities to learn and cope. If you can do this, you'll have much more control over your life.

Context and Content Recasting

Two types of recasting that will change your attitude toward the negative aspects of self-confidence are context and content recasting.

Context recasting refers to your ability to take a negative situation and make it positive in another context. Say your flight is delayed four hours because weather. You could become irritated, as most passengers do, or you could get four hours of work done without interruption. I was recently stuck in Newark, New Jersey, the airport with the most delays in America. Passengers were irate when a United Airlines flight was canceled. Instead of becoming angry, I picked out a chair next to a power plug and started to work on this book. I was actually pretty happy that I had time to get some work done. But a recent BizTravel news report showed that only 15 percent of travelers take time to work or get things done while they travel. Most sleep or simply stare into space.

I have written four books while traveling on airplanes. I could not have accomplished this if all my flights had been on time, nor could I have accomplished it if I hadn't taken advantage of the extra time that became available to me.

Even so, recasting is more than making lemons into lemonade. It is thinking of your experiences as challenges and turning them into benefits.

Once upon a time the 3M Corporation had trouble with the durability of one of their adhesive products. The adhesive could not bond materials permanently, although it did make them adhere temporarily. One researcher used recasting and put just a little bit of adhesive on the back of a piece of paper to make it stick to nearly any surface. Was there an application this adhesive could be used for? You guessed it—Post-its were born.

Here is another example of a context recast:

There once was a farmer who owned an old mule. The mule fell into the farmer's well. The farmer heard the mule braying but after assessing the situation, he decided that neither the mule nor the well was worth the trouble of saving. Instead, he called his neighbors together. He told them what had happened and enlisted them to help haul dirt to bury the old mule in the well and put him out of his misery.

Initially the old mule was hysterical. But as the farmer and his neighbors continued shoveling and the dirt hit his back, a thought struck him. It suddenly dawned on him that every time a shovel load of dirt landed on his back, he would shake it off and step up. This he did, over and over again. Shake it off and step up . . . Shake it off and step up . . . Shake it off and step up . . .

No matter how distressing the situation seemed, the old mule fought panic and just kept right on shaking it off and stepping up.

It wasn't long before the old mule, battered and exhausted, stepped triumphantly over the wall of that well. What seemed like it would bury him had actually blessed him, all because of the way he handled his adversity.

The second type of recasting, *content recasting*, is the mental act of changing what an event means to you. For example, a Christian looks at death not as the end of life but as a new beginning in the kingdom of heaven.

For a more down-to-earth example, take an entrepreneur who recently went bankrupt selling commodities in Chicago. He now has a successful business that consists of several busy hot-dog shops. He describes his first failure as getting an intense education in running a business.

Think of a project you've been putting off. Maybe it's something like repairing a piece of furniture. You can choose to see the job as taking away from the time you'd otherwise spend watching sports on TV, or you can choose to see yourself working on the repair and listening to the game on the radio and enjoying the experience more than if you had actually been watching TV.

This technique works; you simply have to change the negative image of working on the furniture to one where you're having fun. You can even paint the background of the new image in your favorite color and repaint it to include your whole family helping and telling jokes. If you do this, your attitude toward the dreaded experience *will* change.

If this technique seems unbelievably simplistic, think of the last time you did the gardening or another household chore you'd been putting off. Didn't you avoid it for a long time, only to feel after you'd done it that the experience wasn't so bad after all?

My friend, sports commentator Terry Bradshaw, was a famous quarterback and tried his hand as a motivational speaker. He took what he learned from the field and speaking stage to the TV sports desk. He recast his attitude and image in a positive way that empowered him to achieve his goals. He knew he wasn't as articulate as basketball great John Wooden, nor did he have the speaking flair of Fran Tarkenton, or even the attention to detail of Joe Thiesman, but he did have a huge amount of enthusiasm. So he worked on developing a flair for enthusiastic delivery in a way that every audience would find contagious.

The difference between recasting and just being positive is the permanence with which the new thought lasts. If you replace old negative memories with new positive perspectives, you will be able to keep past events from limiting your future success. This in turn will help you become more self-confident in the future.

Recasting Emotions, Behaviors, and Memories

It is even possible to recast emotions, behaviors, and memories. This technique is based on understanding the neurolinguistic programming (NLP) system developed by researchers John Grinder and Richard Bandler. The theory goes that your unconscious controls how you experience and perceive both past memories and current events. It consequently controls all sorts of habitual behaviors, which frees you to think about more important things. For instance, you don't consciously think about braking your car when you come to a stop sign, but you brake nonetheless. That you unconsciously do so frees you to think consciously about the scenery, people, or conversations around you.

However, such unconscious habits may not always be good for you. In some cases, like dieting, habits may sabotage your self-confidence. I spoke to a woman a couple of years ago who had enormous trouble losing weight. She had tried every diet she could think of, and still nothing worked. After several conversations, I learned she had been raped as a teenager. She still struggled with that memory as well as with the low self-esteem she'd had ever since. She was attractive, but her poor self-image was hard to alter after twenty-five years. Because of this low self-esteem, she found it impossible to lose weight. The extra weight simply confirmed this idea. Being thin violated it, so she was unable to lose the weight.

Like this woman, we need to find ways to influence our unconscious in order to get it to support our goals. To do this, we first need to know how we think.

The NLP system holds that people primarily perceive the world in one of three different ways: in pictures, sounds, or feelings. Picture people make sense of the world by constructing or recalling images in their minds. If they can't make a mental picture of what you're saying, they may have trouble understanding your ideas.

Sound people make decisions largely on the basis of what they hear. They make sense of what they hear based on how things sound. They often talk to themselves in order to understand a message.

Feeling people tend to react viscerally. They get a gut emotion talking to you. They may feel hot or cold about you or an idea after just a few minutes of interaction. Many people call this *intuition*.

If you knew what system you were using to perceive the world, could you be more self-confident? You bet. The following approach focuses on your dominant mode of thought to recast your emotions, behaviors, and memories so they will support your goals, including the ones requiring self-confidence.

Four-Step Approach to Recasting Emotions, Behaviors, and Memories

If you use these steps, you will improve your self-confidence.

1. Identify the pattern of behavior or thought you would like to change. For example, many athletes think in visual terms. Many of my tennis buddies tell me they pick a place on the court to serve to. Then they imagine that spot in their minds as they hit the ball.

If you want to hit a serve differently, you might imagine the spin of the ball after it leaves the racket instead of the mechanics of how to hold the racket and bend your elbow. A slice serve is hit by glancing the racket off the side of the ball. You might imagine glancing the racket off the side of the ball. You could picture the ball being peeled like an orange by your racket. You might also imagine the ball jumping straight up as it lands on the other side of the court. This would give you a very powerful mental image in tennis. It is also an example of how to use visualization in any other task you want to accomplish.

In 1977, I was struggling at a professional tournament in Linz, Austria. I had only competed on clay courts for a few months and still had trouble moving on this unstable surface. My serves didn't have the same kick and speed as on the hard courts I was used to. The clay surface caught the ball and slowed it down. The harder I tried to hit the ball, the more mistakes I made. I lost five games in a row and became desperate.

I had just finished a book by Tim Gallwey entitled *The Inner Game of Tennis*. Gallwey was the Zen master of tennis. His teaching method—which was really NLP before there was NLP—was to focus not on how you hit the ball, but on the result. This technique was totally different from any teaching method used at that time. I was desperate and ready for anything. After all, I was on track to losing the match.

I picked out a pebble on the clay surface where I wanted my serve to land, and just let it rip. My ball landed within inches of the target and aced the German national champion, who was my opponent that day. My next serve was a slice and kicked so high that it caught my opponent totally off guard.

As a result, my service game immediately improved and I won the match, all because I concentrated more on the result, and the goal, than on the method to reach it. Methods are always import-ant, but sometimes we get so stuck in technique that we paralyze ourselves.

2. Use signals from your unconscious to determine the background reason for your unwanted behavior and to help change a habit pat-tern. Most of our habitual behaviors and thoughts are unconscious anyway, so the way to go about this is to make your mind go blank and then pose a question to which you are looking for a yes or no answer. Separate the difference between the background reason for the behavior from the behavior itself. Again, do this by using uncon-scious signals that can be answered with yes and no questions.

3. Identify a new, desirable behavior more in line with your goals. Use your unconscious to help, using yes and no questions as a guide-line.

4. Determine whether the new behavior fits in with who you are without inner conflict. Again, use yes and no questions as a guide-line.

For example, say the woman in our previous example, who had been raped, continued to try to lose weight, but her unconscious didn't support this goal. Using step 1, she would identify her eating habits as the behavior she wanted to change. Being thinner would be the goal to which she was consciously committed.

The next step in this process would be to get a signal from her unconscious about this goal. Again, the key to tapping into your unconscious is to think of questions with yes or no answers, clear your mind, and then pose these questions to your unconscious. The answers, negative or positive, won't come in a word. They will be more of an image or feeling or even what you hear yourself thinking.

This is because some of the most common signals from our unconscious are based in our dominant thought mode. If your most powerful mode is using pictures, be passively aware of signals like images in your mind. Are those images dark, light, or small? Your unconscious may signal you by changing those images. It may make an image smaller, signaling no, or brighter, signaling yes. Some people will even see a flashing *yes* in the mental picture as a response to a question.

If you want to lose weight, can you picture yourself as thin? Is the image pleasing? Is the image of a thin body bright and big, or dim and small? If it's dim and small, your unconscious may not be supporting your weight-loss program.

If your dominant mode is auditory, be aware of noises like ringing or other sounds that become louder in support, or quieter when there is opposition. Can you hear people telling you how thin you look? Or do you hear ridicule because you're too thin, like Calista Flockhart in the 1990s sitcom *Ally McBeal*?

If your most powerful mode is feeling, watch for physical sensations. You might become aware that your fingers are tingling, or your legs might get warmer in response to the questions you ask. You also might get a feeling in your gut. Do you feel warmly excited about being thin, or do you feel more dread as you contemplate the work it will take to lose weight? All of these signals are common, but you may feel others as well. Just remain aware of any signals your unconscious wants to use as you ask for yes or no answers to questions.

You might be thinking how silly it is to pay attention to your dominant thought mode as you evaluate your goals. But you do this all the time. You get a feeling before you buy something. You hear a voice in your head that something may not be right. You visualize problems or get excited about future opportunities. We are just using NLP to tap into the processes you are already using.

Tapping into your unconscious is essential for determining the background reason for any unwanted behavior. Ask your questions, and then be alert for answers that come from your dominant mode. The woman in the example who wanted to lose weight discovered there was a secondary gain to being overweight—diminished attention from men. By asking herself questions, she determined that her unconscious resisted losing weight because being heavy saved her from the pressure of dating.

To get your unconscious to stop protecting you through this secondary behavior, you need to acknowledge what it *has* been doing. Then you need to ask if there are other ways to protect yourself from the perceived threat besides the undesired behavior. Again, use a series of yes and no questions to learn what these alternatives might be.

In the case of the overweight woman, she might have asked her unconscious if she could protect herself from the pressures of dating by deciding not to go out with anyone for a certain period of time.

She could also have asked whether dating was really all that threatening. You see how it goes. Asking these questions occurs in a sort of stream of consciousness in which one question leads to another.

Keep in mind that from time to time all of us have secondary gains from a lack of self-confidence. My tardiness in practicing the trumpet at age twelve grew out of my dislike of the instrument. I was consequently late to lessons and procrastinated practicing, but I was never late to baseball or tennis practice.

Likewise, procrastination in going back to college may lie in an unconscious desire not to leave your job as a waitress or bartender. Maybe you really like this job, even though you don't make enough money at it. The truth is, you don't procrastinate doing the things you love. If you think you want the goal but still procrastinate, you need to get your unconscious involved to find out why.

I once read about a pro golfer who ten years earlier had been ranked in the top twenty in the world. He hadn't won a tournament in the intervening years and thought he had the "yips," a tendency to hit the ball with a jerk without smooth control. It's like trying to be extra careful around expensive china and then nervously breaking it all.

The interviewer asked some probing questions about his family and discovered the golfer's spouse wasn't especially supportive. She wanted him to take a job as a local country-club pro. He felt guilty about all the travel time away from his family, and had trouble committing to his demanding goal enough to get back into the top twenty.

In step 3 of recasting emotions, you must create a new behavior that is in line with your goals. Again, let's use the example of the woman who wanted to lose weight. She found through her unconscious that she had a secondary gain from doing just the opposite.

A solution for her was to change her goal of how much weight she would lose—say ten pounds instead of twenty-five. This way her behavior still changed, her goals were still met, and her unconscious had time to adjust. Thus she would be more able to support further weight loss in the future if she so desired.

In the final step of the four-step approach, you need to make sure the new behavior is in line with your unconscious goals. The woman who wanted to lose weight tried to get a sense of her new self-confidence in the context of "Is this really what I want, consciously and unconsciously?" As she checked her unconscious by using the yes and no questions, she also made a commitment to uncover new ways to take the weight off and keep it off. She then used the unconscious signals she had previously accessed to get her unconscious to embrace her goal. Once she had done all these things, she was ready to work toward achieving her objective, albeit a little at a time.

When you use visualization and recasting, you will find that self-confidence can be like Aladdin's lamp: it can grant you just about anything you wish for. All you have to do is know how to rub the lamp. As the old saying goes, beware what you wish for. You may get it!

Assignments:
Putting Self-Confidence to Work

1. Do the exercise of observing others. Look at a person and then look away. Describe to yourself verbally or in writing what that person looks like without looking back. Be as detailed as possible. Then look again and compare your list with how that person actually looks. As you practice, you will get better at visualization.

2. Think back on a pleasurable experience. See it in your mind. Notice the vividness of the images. Now turn up the intensity of the color, proximity, and brightness. Do you feel even happier and more excited?

Then imagine a bad experience and see if you can turn down the vividness. Make your picture of this experience dimmer. See it off in the distance, black-and-white, dull and fuzzy. Try to do this enough to reduce the bad feelings you attach to this event. Does the different image cause you to think of it as less important and less emotional?

Think of a goal you would like to work toward and, as applicable, use content and context recasting to help reshape your attitude toward achieving this goal. One of my friends wanted to hit a better tennis 2nd serve. It was easy to teach him how to spin the ball. He would have to hit the ball just as hard. But instead of hitting the ball straight on, the idea was to glance the racquet off the side of the ball creating spin. But first, he had to recast his bad past memories of double faulting. It's not enough to tell someone to forget the past. Instead they need to make those past memories less vivid. This will allow the server to swing more freely as if he had no bad habits to protect.

Use the four-step process (page 76) to recast emotions, behaviors, and memories in committing yourself to the goal you identified in the activity above.

Five

Changing Your Beliefs

During a momentous battle, a Japanese general decided to attack even though his army was greatly outnumbered. He was confident they would win, but his men were filled with doubt.

On the way to the battle, the army stopped at a religious shrine. After praying with his men, the general took out a coin and said, "I shall now toss this coin. If it is heads, we shall win. If it is tails, we shall lose. Destiny will now reveal itself."

He threw the coin into the air, and all watched intently as it landed. It was heads. The soldiers were so overjoyed and filled with confidence that they vigorously attacked the enemy and were victorious.

After the battle, a lieutenant remarked to the general, "No one can change destiny."

"Quite right," the general replied as he showed the lieutenant the coin, which had heads on both sides.

A few years ago, a New Jersey family was returning home from out of state after visiting relatives. When they approached the state line, they were shocked by what they saw. On the turnpike was a sign that read, "The State of New Jersey is closed." To make matters worse, a policeman stood next to the sign, apparently enforcing the closure. As the mom and dad exited the car, they stared for a long time at the sign, wondering when the state would reopen. When they finally asked the trooper when they could enter, *Candid Camera* producer Allen Funt walked out, explaining that they were on TV.

Would you fight a difficult battle with the odds stacked against you?
You would if you believed you would win.
Would you fall for something as silly as your state being closed?
The answer is the same: you would if you believed, no matter how ridiculous it might seem upon reflection. As Julius Caesar said over 2000 years ago, "Men willingly believe what they wish."
Unfortunately, some of us, like the parrot in the short joke below, believe when we shouldn't.

Once upon a time, a magician was working on a cruise ship in the Caribbean. The audience was different each week, so the magician allowed himself to do the same tricks over and over again.

There was only one problem: The captain's parrot saw the shows every week and began to understand what the magician did in every trick. Once he understood, he started shouting in the middle of the show, "Look, it's not the same hat!" "Look, he's hiding the flowers under the table!" "Hey, why are all the cards the ace of spades?"

The magician was furious but was unable to do anything about the parrot; it belonged to the captain, after all.

One day the ship had an accident and sank. The magician found himself on a piece of wood in the middle of the ocean with the parrot by his side. They stared at each other with hate, but neither uttered a word. This went on for several days.

After a week the parrot finally said, "OK, I give up. What'd you do with the boat?"

As this story makes clear, beliefs often have nothing to do with reality. Instead, they are the foundation of the saying, "Whether you think you can or you think you can't, you're right."

This is a good thing. It means we can alter our beliefs at any time to support self-confidence.

A short time ago I was touring Singapore during the religious festival of Thaipusam. This is a Tamil celebration in which the faithful give thanks and offer atonement for spiritual transgressions. During the ceremony, I watched believers from virtually every walk of life pierce their skin by putting long, slender rods in their mouths and then through their cheeks. The surprising fact was that not one of the hundreds who pierced themselves bled.

This is just one example of the force belief can have in our lives, a force that apparently even has control over bodily functions, such as bleeding when wounded.

Think of what the rest of us could accomplish if we could harness our beliefs to this extent. If we had this kind of control, using self-confidence to achieve our goals would be a snap.

It's the kind of belief shown by a young boy on a Little League baseball team. When asked by a latecomer what the score was, the boy replied with a smile, "We're behind fourteen to nothing."

"Really," the latecomer said. "I have to say you don't look very discouraged."

"Discouraged?" the boy asked with a puzzled look on his face. "Why should we be discouraged? We haven't been up to bat yet."

Earlier I discussed how visualizing success can affect our behavior. After all, images power our beliefs as well as the doubt that shakes them. Doubt exists when there's insufficient faith in a belief, but belief exists when there's a commitment to accepting something that may not always be provable.

To demonstrate how our minds represent a belief in doubt, call to mind one of your very strong beliefs. This belief might be religious, ethical, or related to the way you do business. Try to get a visual image of that belief and what it's done for you in the past. You might recall something that you prayed for that came to pass, or a situation in which ethics paid off. Perhaps it's your strong belief in freedom symbolized by the Statue of Liberty, or your belief that good things come to those who wait. This could be symbolized by the image of your grandmother, who, after struggling through the accidental death of the abusive man she'd married at nineteen, met and married the loving, supportive man who became your grandfather.

Now try to picture something you doubt. This should be something that may or may not be true. You might think of extraterrestrial beings and represent them in your mind with a picture of a flying saucer. Or you might think of your secret desire to be the head of your department at work. You could envision a large, sunny office with a cherry-wood desk.

Now notice the visual differences in the pictures that represent your belief and your doubt. You probably see the belief picture as big, detailed, bright, and colorful, while the picture of what you doubt is probably much smaller, fuzzier, and maybe only in black-and-white. If you pay attention to your emotional and physical processes, you'll probably notice that when you visualize an important belief, you breathe slowly and deeply. Your hands may get warmer as the blood flow increases in your body.

When you experience doubt, you become stressed. Your breathing will become more shallow, and your hands will grow colder and clammy. This is one reason why people who believe in something are so much more courageous than those in doubt. Strong beliefs can make us brave to the point that we are even willing to give our lives, whereas very few feel passionate about things they doubt. How else can we explain the willingness of Islamic extremists to offer themselves as suicide bombers? I haven't met many passionate atheists, have you? I have met a few who don't believe in God, but not many who would die for that belief.

The great thing about belief is that it's always a choice. We can choose beliefs that limit us or beliefs that create power in our lives.

Let's say you want to stop smoking, but you've tried and been unsuccessful. Did you believe from the start that you could accomplish your goal? Did you expect to be successful in your mind?

Think of the power you'd have to take on the goal of quitting smoking, losing weight, or completing a report if you believed from the start that you could do it well. All along you'd approach the goal from a position of success instead of doubt. That belief in your own ability would serve to build your self-confidence.

Give it some thought. Then use the two following exercises to try to change the way you approach your goal, whatever it might be.

1. List an outcome you'd like to achieve. Under it write all the things you know about yourself that will help turn this outcome into reality. As you develop your list, think about whether

you have the determination and drive to complete the task. Remind yourself of your positive traits that will support your success in achieving the goal. Chances are, you already have the talent and ability to accomplish what you want. All you need is to strengthen your internal belief and forget about the things that might hold you back. Review this list every time you doubt your ability to finish a task. This will help shore up your belief in your ability to reach any goal you set.

2. Review the positive traits you identified above and imagine yourself applying them to your outcome. Make a picture of each. Thoughts about these supportive actions should be large, bright, and vivid. Any negative thought should be dim, black, and small. This will reduce the effect of doubt.

It's easier to use beliefs if you understand where they come from. Beliefs don't develop because someone hits us on the head one day telling us what we can and can't believe. Rather, they come from four main sources: our surroundings, what we discover intellectually, our experiences, and our hopes and expectations.

Surroundings

You know that childhood has a great effect on your success later in life. If you grew up in a lower-middle-class neighborhood, it might be hard for you to achieve great wealth in your life. This is due to your unconscious belief that just paying the bills is a struggle. But if your name were DuPont, Rockefeller, or Rothschild, your expectations and beliefs would be quite different. You would be comfortable around money because your parents always were. And they would have taught you how to manage it.

Or possibly not. Think about the Vanderbilts. My wife and I took a vacation recently to the Vanderbilt estate in Asheville, North Carolina. In 1810, the first Vanderbilt, Cornelius, borrowed $100 from his mother to buy a ferry in New York. Later he built a shipping line and made his real money in railroads. The family was worth $300 billion at their zenith, in today's dollars. But in only three generations, the heirs were not worth even $1 million each. Some say they squandered the money. I think it's more than that. I think the Vanderbilts didn't teach their heirs the lessons of how to manage it. By spending just 4 percent of the fortune every year, they could have maintained and even grown their wealth.

Ask yourself, are the outcomes you desire now consistent with the surroundings you experienced when you grew up? If they're not, can you cope with the differences in lifestyle these outcomes might bring? If you're a salesperson trying to make more money, do you believe you can cope with the changes that may come with greater wealth? Do you believe you really want money and greater wealth?

You're probably answering an enthusiastic "Yes!" but be careful: if you don't really believe you can or should make a higher income, you'll unconsciously sabotage your self-confidence in your attempt to do so.

To see if your belief is compatible with your goal of making more money, employ a technique called *future belief check*. In your mind, see a visual representation of a specific outcome you desire. Now see an image of yourself with that outcome to determine whether or not you think you deserve it. How vivid can you make that picture? Is it bright? Is it large? Is it colorful? If it isn't, this outcome may not be consistent with your beliefs. You need to either change the outcome or change your belief.

Intellect

The second source of beliefs is our intellect. Here's how to use your intellect to check your beliefs. Take the same outcome you used in the last example. See the picture in your mind, and check to see if you believe you're intelligent enough to achieve that outcome. If your outcome is to complete college, do you believe you're sharp enough to get good grades? Your friends may know that you are, but do *you* know it? Imagine yourself wearing a graduation gown or carrying an armload of books, and check for the vividness, brightness, and size of the image.

Experiences

The third source of belief is our experiences. If you've been successful achieving things in the past, you'll likely be successful in the future. But if you've experienced stumbling blocks or limitations in the past, you may find it difficult to change your expectations for the future. However, it's not impossible.

Let's try the belief check again. Imagine your outcome once more, and next to it envision a past failure. Then try to see the outcome as completed, shored up by your experience of the past. Is that picture vivid, large, and well defined? Will your past experience give you the self-confidence you need to achieve this outcome in the future? The picture and its characteristics will give you a good idea of the answer.

Hopes and Expectations

The fourth source of belief is our hopes and expectations of the future. Unless we hope very strongly for something, this is one of the hardest ways to develop strong beliefs. That's because there are so few tangible things other than faith on which to base future expectations. Even so, most of us probably have a belief right now that when we go to work tomorrow, we'll have a good day. Developing a belief in future success is the lifeblood of any goal, especially in commissioned businesses like sales.

I like to think of the story of little Jamie Scott when I consider hopes and expectations. Jamie was trying out for a part in a school play and had his heart set on being in it, but his mother feared he would not be chosen. After school on the day the parts were awarded, Jamie rushed up to his mom, his eyes shining with pride and excitement. "Guess what, Mom!" he shouted. "I've been chosen to clap and cheer!"

A friend of mine is a classic example of someone whose beliefs come from her intellect and experiences, though not from her surroundings, hopes, or expectations. Suzanne, a happy homemaker in her midthirties, feared flying her entire life. The fact that airplanes are statistically safer than cars was meaningless to her. After all, planes crash, though not often. It didn't help matters that every news article she'd ever seen on the subject had been permanently imprinted on her brain. They solidified her belief that crashes happen more often than they do.

Suzanne is an intelligent woman. She actually used her intellect to rationalize her fear of flying. "Are several tons of steel *supposed* to fly through the air?" she asked. She reasoned that even if there is only one chance in a million that a plane will crash, it would be hers that ends up in a crater. She felt this way even though no one in her family entertains such fears. In fact her parents and siblings enjoy flying.

Because of her fear of flying, on vacations Suzanne and her family have exclusively driven instead of flown, even though they can afford more luxurious trips. She's missed out on a few significant opportunities over the years—a trip to Aruba with friends after college graduation, the honeymoon in Greece her husband had wanted—but all in all, life has gone pretty smoothly.

Finally she was forced to confront her fear, thanks to a family wedding on the other side of the country. It was scheduled alongside her son's hockey tournament. She couldn't miss one or the other, and that meant flying.

Her husband was relieved that the issue is finally being addressed. But as the days before the trip passed by, Suzanne was increasingly fearful. She was having trouble eating and sleeping. Plain and simple, she needed to change her beliefs.

Restructuring Beliefs

As in Suzanne's case, beliefs can be self-sabotaging, especially when they are incorrect or bad for us. It sometimes takes a problem or tragedy to illuminate our knowledge to the point that we can change. The following story illustrates this beautifully.

A man once found the cocoon of a butterfly. He began keeping an eye on it and one day noticed that a small opening had appeared. The man sat and watched for several hours as the butterfly struggled to force its body through the little hole. Then the butterfly seemed to stop making any progress. It appeared as though it had gotten as far as it could and could go no further.

The man decided to help the butterfly. He took a pair of scissors and snipped off the remaining bit of the cocoon. The butterfly emerged easily, but it had a swollen body and small, shriveled wings.

The man continued to watch the butterfly, expecting that at any moment the wings would enlarge and expand to support the body, which would contract in time.

Neither happened! The butterfly spent the rest of its life crawling around with a swollen body and shriveled wings. It never was able to fly.

In his kindness and haste, the man did not understand that the restricting cocoon and the struggle required for the butterfly to get through the tiny opening were nature's way of forcing fluid from the butterfly's body into its wings so that it would be ready for flight once it was free from the cocoon.

Fortunately, sometimes with education and sometimes with self-confidence, we can change our beliefs to support our goals. One way of doing this is the *submodality change technique*, which can help us discover how beliefs can be diffused and reformulated in a new way.

To grasp this technique, envision a belief you hold. Play with each pictorial difference in this belief. Try to change the brightness, color, vividness, size, and other features that you may notice. Make sure the belief is very specific.

For example, make your belief about future wealth a big house in the countryside. Make your belief about becoming a better golfer into a picture of you winning a major tournament in a couple of years. If your belief is that you will receive an advanced education, you might imagine a cap and gown. Use whatever represents your belief in the most visual and tangible way you can.

Now call up a picture of the belief that you want to change and alter its characteristics. If your belief is large, make your picture small. If your belief is bright, make your picture dim. If it's detailed, make your picture fuzzy. If your belief is stable, make your picture flash. If your belief has color, change it to black-and-white. With each of these steps, notice the psychological and emotional changes you undergo.

Next, deliberately weaken the belief you want to change. Once you make this picture dim, small, and in black-and-white, you'll start to see it flash as it fades away. If you leave that frame empty with no picture to replace it, you'll experience anxiety. Instead replace it with a belief you want: You have the power to lose as many pounds as you want. You have the ability to fire a staff person who is unproductive, late, and rude. You have the power to overcome your habit of not listening to the people around you. Weaken the doubt image of yourself, eliminate it, and then replace it with the image of yourself practicing attentiveness.

My friend Suzanne was able to do this. She knew she wanted to overcome her fear of flying. She began by envisioning the belief that she and her husband would have a wonderful time on the coast of Maine, watching their niece get married and celebrating with her sister and relatives. She imagined the lobster boil on the eve of the wedding. She made that picture bright, vivid, and large. She was so successful at conjuring up the experience of eating fresh New England clam chowder that her mouth watered.

Then she called up the belief she wanted to change: the belief that her plane would crash. Initially this belief was bright, vivid, and large in her mind. She deliberately changed the characteristics of the picture, making it dim, fuzzy, and flashing away in the distance. She replaced that picture with a new belief: that her plane would safely and successfully take off, fly, and land on the ground. In her mind, she saw the airplane soaring gracefully through the sky. She saw herself smiling, holding her husband's hand, and accepting peanuts from a gracious flight attendant. She actually felt the plane landing on the ground, bumping gently, and then gliding to a halt. She saw herself walking down the steps of the plane and collecting her luggage.

Suzanne was getting close to successfully changing her beliefs, but she wasn't quite there yet. The next step of the submodality change technique is to frame the new belief, not in terms of an end result but in terms of the process or the ability that will help you achieve and gain your goal. For Suzanne, this might mean seeing herself able to fly without anxiety and traveling to places around the world she had always dreamed about.

The last step of the submodality change technique is to do an emotional stability check. Determine if there's any way your new belief could be a problem for you. Could it cause you any emotional conflict in the future? In Suzanne's case, flying more and traveling may take her away from loved ones she cherishes. Perhaps traveling more would not be something she would enjoy in the long term. If she traveled too much, it would take her away from people she loves spending time with.

In other words, just because you are able to eliminate a fear doesn't mean you should do it. I may be able to eliminate a fear of bungee jumping, but that doesn't mean I should engage in that activity. This relates to self-confidence in that you don't need to be confident about everything. Some apprehension is good, as in the case of the blind discus thrower in a crowded stadium: the fans stay attentive.

If a new belief is good for you, then proceed. If you're not sure, use a concept called *congruency*. It's incredibly effective in helping you decide whether a belief is emotionally good for you.

Congruency basically says that you should evaluate a new belief from all three thought processes—seeing, hearing, and feeling—to determine if it will create any inner conflict or anxiety for you. For example, if your new belief is to be more assertive when people are taking advantage, you might see yourself responding differently. As you plug into the three neurolinguistic thought processes, you'll *see* yourself tough and assertive, perhaps in the way you stand, walk, or even sit. Auditorily, you'll *hear* yourself talking in a very assertive way. Kinesthetically, you'll *feel* more confidence and greater strength in your communications with people. You'll be more assertive in letting others know how you feel.

On the other hand, if your boss is uncomfortable with your being more assertive, you might want to avoid acting this way with her. A compromise might be to weaken the current belief that you need to be assertive with everyone and instead limit your assertiveness to people who take advantage of you.

Let's try the whole thing from the beginning. Start with a goal that on some level you doubt you can achieve or sustain, for example pursuing a law degree. Your belief could be that the material will be too demanding or that you're too old. As you look at that belief, you should try to turn it into doubt by testing each mode of thought. Try to make it small, dim, and fuzzy. Any sounds connected with it should become soft, then inaudible. You should also turn down the strength of your feelings about it, perhaps by using the disassociation technique we discussed earlier.

Use the submodality change technique to weaken your doubt you feel. Turn the image of your learning difficulty into a flashing picture. When the flashing begins, immediately replace it with a picture of yourself successfully studying and concentrating on the information in front of you. See yourself smiling, reading a book, as you gain new, useful information. (This would be a more positive representation than an image of working long, hard hours.) Bring the image to the forefront and make it vivid, colorful, and detailed. Notice how the frame of the picture gets bigger and the image gets brighter and sharper. You might hear soft classical or jazz music in the background.

Notice the physiological changes you experience. You should be smiling, feeling more joyous, more encouraged, and happier about your goal. You should feel as if a load has been lifted from your mind for one very good reason: two strong conflicting beliefs about the same thing can't exist. You just have to weaken one belief before the other one can replace it. This technique short-circuits the process of eliminating doubts and nonsupportive beliefs.

Now frame the new belief. To develop enough self-confidence to earn a law degree, see yourself as able to learn, having a great memory, and being a fast reader. When the going gets tough, refer to this mental picture. It will reinforce the self-confidence you need to carry on.

Lastly, do an emotional stability check on your new belief. If need be, use the technique of congruency to evaluate your new belief from all three thought processes: seeing, hearing, and feeling. In gaining the confidence to pursue a law degree, you would imagine what the degree looks like, sounds like, and feels like, while at the same time making sure that being a lawyer is congruent with how you feel.

I have a good friend who doesn't like being a lawyer. If he were to pursue more education for a new specialty, no matter how he was able to change his beliefs, it wouldn't change the fact that he doesn't enjoy practicing law. Congruency means that your beliefs have to correspond with what you enjoy and love already, as well as with what you *don't* enjoy. In short, make sure the things you want to be self-confident about are in line with the things you really want.

You can also try replacing nonsupportive beliefs and doubts with supportive beliefs. You do this by moving from a belief to doubt, to contrasting the two, to finally testing the new belief.

Say you're good with people and believe that as a personnel manager you could effectively help your coworkers be more productive. You might represent this by seeing an image of yourself working side-by-side with one employee, and then another, giving directions that will help develop win-win situations for both of you.

Now think of a doubt. Suppose your outcome is to become a department head in your company but, in spite of how good you are with people, you're afraid you don't have the confidence to lead thirty individuals. How would you represent this in your mind? It might be a picture of yourself acting confused and disorganized, not knowing what to do next.

Look at the differences between your pictures of belief and doubt. Notice the changes in brightness, vividness, color, and fuzziness. Notice how big each picture is and whether it flashes.

Next, test each of these submodality differences, one at a time, to discover which is the most powerful in changing the doubt picture to belief. Perhaps going from a vivid to a dim picture has the greatest power. Perhaps changing the color of the picture from bright primary tones to a dull grey does the trick and causes the doubt picture to flash or even fade away. Any one of these characteristics could do the trick; you just have to test each one.

Finally, make sure you have a new belief in your mind with which to replace the doubt. If you doubt that you are confident enough to become a good manager, you need to replace that doubt with a new belief that gives you that power. See yourself learning ideas and concepts quickly. Make an image of yourself flying through books that seem complex to others. As you do this, remember to think of the new belief in positive terms only. Also, think of the belief as a process rather than as a goal or a delusion. (A delusion would be having the belief that you can be wealthy and then seeing yourself as the richest person in the world.)

The process of changing beliefs is very simple. Through the coming days, test your new beliefs to make sure the emotions and associations connected with them are consistent with the changes that have occurred. Do this by testing the visual representation of each of your beliefs. What does your belief look like after several days? Is it still vivid? Is it still big, colorful, and in the center of the picture frame? Does it still have all the characteristics that were there when you made it? You might have to reinforce it by going through these exercises again, but with practice you'll find the new belief integrated into your way of life.

Just remember that beliefs and goals need to be in harmony. If they are, you'll be able to work miracles, the way the great violinist Itzhak Perlman did at the beginning of one concert. I've not been able to discover who wrote the account that follows, but it is an incredible reminder of how powerful beliefs can be.

On November 18, 1995, Itzhak Perlman came on stage to give a concert at Avery Fisher Hall at Lincoln Center in New York City. If you've ever been to a Perlman concert, you know that getting on stage is no small achievement for him. He was stricken with polio as a child, so he has braces on both legs and walks with the aid of two crutches. To see him walk across the stage one step at a time is an awesome sight. He walks painfully, yet majestically, until he reaches his chair. Then he slowly sits down, puts his crutches on the floor, undoes the clasps on his legs, tucks one foot back, and extends the other foot forward. Then he bends down and picks up the violin, puts it under his chin, nods to the conductor, and proceeds to play.

The audience is used to this ritual. They sit quietly while he makes his way across the stage to his chair. They remain reverently silent while he undoes the clasps on his legs. They wait until he is ready to play.

But this time, something went wrong. Just as he finished the first few bars, one of the strings on his violin broke. You could hear it snap—it went off like gunfire across the room. There was no mistaking what that sound meant.

There was also no mistaking what he had to do. People who were there that night said, "We figured he would have to get up, put on the clasps again, pick up the crutches, and limp his way off stage, to either find another violin or else find another string for this one."

But he didn't. Instead he waited a moment, closed his eyes, and then signaled the conductor to begin again. The orchestra began, and he played from where he had left off. And he played with such passion and such power and such purity as the audience had never heard before.

Everyone knows it is impossible to play a symphonic violin work with just three strings. I know that and you know that, but that night, Itzhak Perlman refused to know that. You could see him modulating, changing, recomposing the piece in his head. At one point, it sounded as if he were detuning the strings to get new sounds from them that they had never made before.

When he finished, there was an awesome silence in the room. And then people rose and cheered. There was an extraordinary outburst of applause from every corner of the auditorium. We were all on our feet, screaming and cheering, doing everything we could to show how much we appreciated what he had done.

He smiled, wiped the sweat from his brow, raised his bow to quiet us, and then said, not boastfully but in a quiet, pensive, reverent tone, "You know, sometimes it is the artist's task to find out how much music you can still make with what you have left."

Beliefs are powerful. Use the positive beliefs you have and change those that are self-sabotaging to achieve ever greater self-confidence in your life.

Assignments:
Putting Self-Confidence to Work

1. Take one of the goals and outcomes you wrote down earlier and list both the positive and negative beliefs that either limit or empower you to achieve that goal and outcome. Then replace each of the old, nonsupportive beliefs with new beliefs that will support your goals. Use the submodality change technique to do this.

2. Write down three of your beliefs that are based on future hopes and expectations and put a check mark next to those beliefs that support you in achieving a goal you have set for yourself. Then perform the belief check we've already outlined. What do you already believe about your abilities to achieve your goal? What part are you anxious about?

If your goal is to get an MBA, a belief that would support that goal might be knowing that you're able to learn quickly and have a desire to gain knowledge. If your goal is to earn enough money to buy a house, your belief might be that you possess the ability to save money and don't need to live from paycheck to paycheck. Developing self-confidence is easier than you think.

Six

Metapatterns

One way you can boost self-confidence is through meta-patterns. The concept of metapatterns explains how we process information. They are like internal computer programs that enable us to generalize, store information, pay attention to, or ignore certain bits of information that can affect our attitudes and perceptions. Metapatterns are the states of mind we automatically access as we work to achieve what we want out of life.

Once upon a time, an exasperated mother whose son was always getting into mischief, finally asked him, "How do you expect to get into heaven?"

The boy thought it over and said, "Well, I'll just run in and out and in and out and keep slamming the door until St. Peter says, 'For heaven's sake, Jimmy, come in or stay out!'"

Jimmy, like most children, has well-developed metapatterns and behavior patterns. The two can be closely linked. When my daughter Caroline was eight years old, she found that she couldn't compete with her sister Catherine, then ten, intellectually or physically, but she did have other resources: she could cry and whine. When she wanted something or felt her sister was taking advantage, she would do a sort of cry/whine that was very effective in helping her get what she wanted. After all, Mom and Dad always came running.

Catherine also found a behavior that worked in helping her get her way: aggression. When she wanted something, Catherine would just take it from her sister, which in turn caused her to cry and whine.

Getting into mischief, crying/whining, and resorting to aggression are just three of the metapatterns kids commonly use. Adults use these metapatterns too, though less often than children. Adult metapatterns are very complex and more effective than those of children. Metapatterns are more than a set of preferences. They're the drives that keep us moving in a certain direction, whether it's toward or away from something. Some of us move toward heavy physical exercise, for example, and spend time in gyms or outdoors jogging or walking. Others move away from strenuous physical activity. Still others move towards the arts by going to concerts, museums, or the ballet, while others shun everything except hoedowns in the barn.

Human beings display five types of metapatterns. Knowing what they are, how they influence us, and how to use them to our advantage is one highly effective way of achieving self-confidence.

Metapattern One: Moving Toward or Away

If somebody asked you what you wanted out of your career, your family, or your life, would you tell them what you wanted or what you didn't want? Likewise, does your cup tend to be half full or half empty? This tendency to move toward or away makes up the first type of metapattern.

Someone with a moving-toward metapattern would answer the question in terms of what they wanted. Someone with a moving-away metapattern would answer the question in terms of what they didn't want.

To determine whether your metapattern is one of moving toward or away, think about how you tend to answer the typical question most spouses and parents ask when you get home from work or school: "How was your day?" If your tendency is to answer "Great!" or some such variation, your metapattern is one of moving toward. If your tendency is to answer somewhat negatively, such as "Not so good" or "OK, I guess" or "Rotten, as usual," your metapattern is one of moving away.

I'm always amazed when I ask someone how they are and hear, "Things could be worse" or "So-so" and then hear others say, "Great!" or "Couldn't be better." Recognize the moving-toward and moving-away metapatterns?

You can also ask yourself how you decided to buy or rent your last home. Respond out loud if you can. If you answer that you decided on your current home because it had a beautiful view with a big yard or old, graceful trees or something else positive about it, your metastate is one of moving toward an option. If you answer that it was the best of a bad lot or you liked it at first but wouldn't move there again because the living room is too small, your metastate is one of moving away.

Or ask yourself how you decided to buy your last car. If you answer that it was the only one you could afford, your metastate is one of moving away. If you describe all the great things about it, your metastate is one of moving toward.

Recently I asked a friend what she desired from a date. She spent almost half an hour telling me what she didn't want in a man. She didn't want someone who was poor, who wasn't able to show her attention, who didn't spend a lot of time with her, and who wasn't tall, dark, and handsome. I understood what she didn't want, but I was still confused about what she did want. I even asked her the same question again. She said, "I just told you, didn't I?"

Metapattern Two: Frame of Reference

The second metapattern that makes up our attitude is *frame of reference*. This frame of reference is either *internal* or *external*. For example, how do you know when you've done a good job on a project? If you know you've done well only when others tell you that you have, your frame of reference is external. If you have a gut feeling that your work is good no matter what anyone says, your frame of reference is internal. Pretty self-explanatory, isn't it?

I was thinking about beginning my MBA program a few years back when a friend said, "Are you nuts? You already have a PhD. You are really successful. You are already overeducated. You won't have as much time at home and won't be able to spend as much time with your kids. This is crazy; the time it will take you to study won't be worth it."

This reaction really threw me, and for a time I didn't enter the program. If you have an external frame of reference, other people can knock you out of self-confidence. If you have an internal frame of reference, you are more likely to stay focused on your goal.

To be more self-confident, we need to have a stronger internal frame of reference. To strengthen your internal frame, once you've set an outcome for yourself, measure every action you take against that outcome. This will help you resist external forces that might draw you away from it.

Another way to strengthen your internal frame of reference is to use the belief representations we talked about earlier. Try right now to reaccess that picture of the belief that supports an outcome you have in mind.

For instance, if you're working on that MBA, imagine yourself breezing through graduate studies at the top of your class. Try to pay very close attention to the brightness, the size, and the vividness of the picture. Now go back to thinking about your outcome—getting the MBA. That outcome will occur if you stay internally focused. Then, every time you hear doubting comments, call to mind the picture of the belief that shows you have the ability to get that MBA.

Metapattern Three: Sorting

The third metapattern involves how emotions are sorted. This basically concerns how we see ourselves in relation to others. If you sort only by yourself, you might be a self-absorbed, arrogant egotist. On the other hand, if you consistently sort by others, you might be an emotional martyr.

How does the metapattern of sorting affect self-confidence? Again, as with external or internal frames of reference, if you sort by others exclusively, your metapattern may sabotage your chances of becoming self-confident and staying focused on your objectives and outcomes.

I knew a man who consistently shot himself in the foot in achieving a high level of wealth because he was unable to control the degree to which he sorted by others.

Warren Harvey was brilliant and a hard worker. He was also a well-liked, generous man who could be counted on to quietly slip you a twenty-dollar bill from his pocket or to buy you lunch at the local café if you were on hard times.

His dream was to own his own real-estate company, and by the time he was forty years old, he had achieved this dream. Times were good, business was booming, and Harvey soon employed a dozen or so support staff. He had also taken on a number of partners, individuals whose company he greatly enjoyed and who also desired great wealth.

Unfortunately, not all of the new employees or partners had Harvey's brilliance or work ethic, even though they were pleasant people to work with. When the economy took a nosedive and the real-estate market fell off, Harvey worked harder than ever and continued to bring money into the company. But the money he brought in did just that: It went into the company to support all the various staff who were not earning their own keep. It did not go into Harvey's pocket, though Harvey spent money as though it did.

The years went by, and the pattern continued. It wasn't long before Harvey had dug himself into a financial hole so deep that his wife had to go to work to help support the family. Twenty years later, she's still working to help extricate the family from debt, while Harvey's business goes on much the same as before, employing numerous staff who cost a lot and who bring in very little money, with Harvey working endless hours and bringing in just enough to keep them all going. Ironically, closing up shop and working for himself would bring him a comfortable level of wealth, but he can't bring himself to do it. He feels responsible for all these people he's employed and doesn't want to let them down.

While the story of Warren Harvey might make it look like sorting by self is best, the best of both worlds is to be somewhere in the middle, leaning toward the sorting-by-self side. You can't and shouldn't ignore others, but it's important to keep focused on what you want and need.

Here are some questions to determine whether you sort by others or by self: What do you like best about your job? If you answer that it pays well or the hours are good or another self-centered reason, you are sorting by self. On the other hand, if meeting wonderful people is the reason you like your job, you probably sort by others.

Likewise, do you like to work with others or by yourself? If you answer by yourself, you probably sort by self. The opposite goes for you if you work best with others, but remember that sorting by others can harm your self-confidence. After all, if you have a deadline to get a project done but someone needs to talk to you, sorting by others could affect your ability to meet that deadline.

You can learn to sort by self by using a reward system. For example, if you have a deadline and you're assertive enough to tell your friend that you'd love to talk after the project is over, you could give yourself a reward of golf on the weekend or a dinner for two.

Metapattern Four: Necessity or Possibility

The fourth metapattern that affects our attitude is the tendency to be motivated by necessity or possibility. A heartwarming story about a little girl who is clearly motivated by possibility rather than necessity goes like this:

Sarah, ten years old, wears a brace all the time because she was born with a muscle missing in her left foot. She came home one beautiful spring day to tell her father she had just competed in field day at school, where they had lots of races and other competitive events.

Because of her leg support, her father's mind raced as he tried to think of encouragement for Sarah, things he could say to her about not letting this get her down. Before he could get a word out, she said, "Daddy, I won two of the races!"

Her father couldn't believe it! And then Sarah said, "I had an advantage." Ah . . . The father knew it. He figured she must have been given a head start or some other kind of physical advantage. But before he could say anything, Sarah said, "Daddy, I didn't get a head start. My advantage was I had to try harder!"

A good way to discover how somebody is motivated is, again, to ask why they bought their house. If they said they needed a five-bedroom house because they have four kids or because they needed a study to work in, they are probably motivated by necessity. Likewise, station-wagon owners and van drivers are more likely motivated by necessity than by possibility, while those driving VW convertibles or Porsches are more likely motivated by possibility than necessity.

Possibility people are motivated less by what they *have* to do than by what they *want* to do. They see a wide variety of choices, experiences, and options in life. They're very interested in knowing what they *can* have rather than what they *should* have.

For self-confidence, it's good to have a mixture of both tendencies. While your goals should take into account the necessities of staying committed, they should also include thinking by possibility—looking at new ways of reaching your outcomes more quickly.

Metapattern Five: Work Style

The fifth and last type of metapattern involves your particular work style. There are three kinds of work-style metapatterns. The first is *independent*, the second is *cooperative*, and the third relates to *proximity*.

1. The **independent metapattern** is displayed by those who get a great deal of enjoyment from working on their own. These individuals like to work by themselves and take full credit for it. They're the sort who wish less to become part of a group than to run a group, and they may have difficulty working with other people.

For example, if your metapattern leans toward the independent side, but you decide to campaign to be president of the local parent-teacher association (PTA), you might be in trouble. Think of how bad this could be for you! As president, you are responsible to your constituency. You also have to lead and interact with those who hold positions in the PTA. You're independent and controlling, but you're going to have to work with others to get what you want done. Can you see the sparks flying already as you hear yourself telling them, "It's my way or the highway"?

You might be better off simply writing letters to the leadership of the PTA telling them how to better run their organization. At least then you wouldn't have to try to work with them.

2. Individuals with a **cooperative metapattern** want to be part of a decision-making body. They want to share responsibilities and activities. They're the sort of people who may not like to make a decision on their own so much as they like to get agreement from others before committing themselves.

If one of your goals is to read every evening, but your metapattern includes a cooperative, interpersonal mind-set, you might find it difficult to spend much time by yourself. The solution might be to read one hour each evening before joining friends.

Take another example: Every January I go skiing with about forty doctors from around the U.S. who form the Blue River Trauma Society (BRTS). We helicopter in to the rugged mountain range called the Cariboos in British Columbia. You have to be an advanced or expert skier to attempt this kind of risky adventure, but all the docs in the group have a wonderful time. One day, one of us wanted to go into the lodge because it was too cold. He complained a little and could have gone in anytime on his own, but instead he tried to get agreement from the four other people in the helicopter before he committed himself to stopping for the day. To see the cooperative metapattern played out in front of my eyes was both amusing and unmistakable.

3. The final category in this group consists of individuals who display a **proximity metapattern**. This is a mixture of the first two types. These people like to work with others while maintaining control over a project. If this is your metapattern, your attitude might be influenced by the kinds of projects you're working on.

A good example of the proximity metapattern again comes from the BRTS group. The group's leader, an orthopedic surgeon named John Campbell from Bozeman, Montana, organizes the group every year for very little compensation. He is a member of the group, but also the organizer. It is fun to watch him ride roughshod over what often looks like an ill-behaved fraternity, yet still revels in the group's activities.

This proximity metapattern seems to include the best of both worlds: you get to enjoy others' company, but you have the ability to run things or simply be by yourself.

Has this metapattern concept begun to sink in? Let's test it and see. Think about the last few U.S. presidents, beginning with George W. Bush. Which metapatterns do you think he displayed? Does he seem to move toward or away from issues? This is debatable, but he seemed to move away from many divisive issues in the beginning of his presidency until terrorism took front stage. Then he moved toward it, as the old saying goes, "like white on rice."

Barack Obama seemed to have a moving-away metapattern. In the latter part of his presidency, he was accused of not making decisions instead of making the wrong ones.

Here's a tougher one: During Bill Clinton's scandals, do you think he sorted by himself or by others? He seemed to be watching the polls pretty carefully in the heat of his troubles, especially regarding the Monica Lewinsky issue. He also appeared to find amazing confidence after a poll showed the American people didn't want to see him impeached merely for an extramarital affair. Right or wrong, sorting by others seems to have enabled him to weather the calls for his resignation.

Finally, do you think Ronald Reagan used an independent or proximity metapattern? From presidential historians, we have learned that he seemed to be great in front of crowds but didn't particularly like the day-to-day cabinet meetings. He was also famous for leaving much of the responsibility for various governmental workings to those he trusted. In spite of this, no one has claimed he wasn't a great leader. Rather, the argument has been made that sometimes leadership is manifested in motivating large groups rather than in interactions with only a few. Reagan was not a pragmatist who wanted a well-functioning government. He was an ideologue. He was an independent metapattern person. He wanted agreement but wasn't guided by it. He was focused toward his own version of low tax, limited government conservatism.

It should be obvious by now that the metapatterns we display have a great bearing on whether we'll be successfully self-confident. Because of this, either the approaches we take need to fit well into the metapatterns we already possess or we need to alter our metapatterns.

The good news is, we can change our metapatterns by distorting, deleting, or generalizing incoming information. We all do this to some extent anyway. Why not consciously capitalize on it to help maintain self-confidence? As George Bernard Shaw once said, "If you can't get rid of the skeleton in your closet, you'd best teach it to dance."

For example, if you tend to sort by self, but a friend has a big office party coming up that she wants you to attend with her, you can build your confidence by distorting the incoming information that causes you anxiety and telling yourself, "I will not be the only person at this party who doesn't enjoy big get-togethers. There will be someone else hanging out in the corner or the kitchen, and I will be able to escape there too when I need a break."

In another example, say you are an individual with a moving-away metapattern whose desired outcome is to get an MBA. You read an article that academic degrees of this type are no longer as important as they once were for getting a better job. Your automatic response might be to say, "Why am I killing myself working an eight-hour job and going to class at the same time?"

Instead, delete the information that favors your metapattern and rationalize that there will always be great opportunities for qualified people, more so now than ever.

Likewise, if you're having trouble staying on your diet, you could delete that bit of information. Tell yourself that a little sacrifice now will be nothing compared to the joy you will have with a new body after a couple of months of dieting.

You can also generalize incoming information to help alter a particular metapattern. If your frame of reference is external and your wife has a business meeting out of town for the second weekend in a row, don't tell yourself, "This really stinks! I can't believe she's leaving again so soon! Now what am I going to do?" Instead say to yourself, "Despite how it appears right now, this doesn't happen very often, and it means she's really doing well in the company. I'm proud of her, and I know she will miss me too, but this will be a good chance for me to get some much-needed work done around the house."

It can take some time to get into the habit of working with our existing metapatterns. Traumatic situations, though not desired, can cut through the chase and help us change our metapatterns quickly, as the following story suggests:

Sometime ago a man punished his five-year-old daughter for wasting a roll of expensive gold wrapping paper. Money was tight, and he became upset when the child pasted the gold paper on a box to put under the Christmas tree.

Nevertheless, the little girl brought the gift to her father the next morning and said, "This is for you, Daddy."

The father was embarrassed by his earlier reaction, but his anger flared again when he found the box was empty. He spoke to the child in a harsh manner. "Don't you know, young lady, that when you give someone a present, there's supposed to be something inside the package?"

The little girl looked up at him with tears in her eyes and said, "Oh, Daddy, it's not empty. I blew kisses into it until it was full."

The father was crushed. He fell on his knees and put his arms around his little girl and begged her to forgive him for his unnecessary anger.

An accident took the life of the child only a short time later. It is said that the father was a changed man forever. He kept that gold box by his bed for all the remaining years of his life. Whenever he was discouraged or faced difficult problems, he would open the box and take out an imaginary kiss and remember the love of the child who had put it there.

Using Metapatterns Successfully

Regardless of which metapatterns you display, to use them successfully, you need to keep in mind the following four tips:

1. Recognize which metapatterns you possess. For example, if you have a metapattern that's typically moving toward things, then thinking about a great body is a better way to slim down than to think about losing weight. If your metapattern is moving away, thinking about actually losing weight would be a more effective way for you to achieve your outcome.

2. Use your frame of reference, whether internal or external, to support your goal and outcome. If your frame of reference is external, telling yourself you'd be a great candidate for a weight-loss program would be a good idea because of your concern about other's opinions.

3. Change your belief systems to best utilize your existing meta-patterns. As you may find, metapatterns can be difficult to change. If yours is one of moving toward rather than moving away, and your diet outcomes are focused on losing twenty-five pounds, there's a conflict. To make your metapatterns and outcomes congruent, you can use a belief in your ability to eat two small meals a day instead of three large meals. That's a way to modify the outcome to best use the existing metapattern.

4. Monitor yourself through your self-confidence change program. Make sure you're actively focusing on information that supports your most effective metapattern. If your frame of reference tends to be external, make sure not to let others discourage you. If your frame of reference is internal, you may want to insulate yourself from others and not tell them what your goals are.

I tend to move away from things rather than towards them. Another of my metapatterns is necessity rather than possibility. During the final stretch of my MBA studies, I found the course on managerial accounting so difficult I actually asked my CPA for help. John told me there are two types of people in the world: those who have a mind for numbers and those who don't. He advised me to drop out of the course and take another prerequisite, but I had invested too much time and trouble for that. Getting an A+ in the course didn't motivate me, but getting a D did. As soon as I was able to see how near I was to failing, I jumped into high gear, studying and cramming almost twelve hours a day until the final exam. I ended up with an A+ for the course, but it wasn't because I was trying to do well. I was trying not to fail.

Knowing my metapatterns enables me to concentrate on what is naturally appealing. For example, there are some goals in my life I want to just go out and grab. These include a better serve and forehand in tennis. There are also some problems I want to move away from. These include traffic tickets, flight delays, and behavior problems with my kids. Likewise, I love to speak to groups, but I hate airline flights. The carriers are increasingly passenger-unfriendly, the security is tighter, and it is becoming lunacy to spend ninety minutes waiting to get through a security line.

It would be easy to say that my career is too tough. (Recognize the moving-away metapattern?) Instead I distort the airline experiences in favor of remembering the great places I travel to and the wonderful people I'm privileged to address.

In the final analysis, it's good to be aware of our metapatterns for one overriding reason: we can put them to work for us instead of against us, as the young executive in the following story eventually managed to do.

A young and successful executive was traveling down a neighborhood street, as usual going a bit too fast in his new Jaguar. He loved to drive fast, loved the rush of adrenaline it gave him. He was watching for kids darting out from between parked cars and slowed down when he thought he saw something.

As his car passed, no children appeared. Instead, a brick smashed into the Jag's side door. The man slammed on the brakes and drove the Jag back to the spot where the brick had been thrown.

The angry driver then jumped out of the car, grabbed the nearest kid, and pushed him up against a parked car, shouting, "What was that all about? What the heck are you doing? That's a new car and that brick you threw is going to cost a lot of money. Why did you do it?"

The young boy was apologetic. "Please mister . . . Please, I'm sorry. I didn't know what else to do. I threw the brick because no one would stop."

With tears dripping down his face, the youth pointed to a spot just around a parked car. "It's my brother," he said. "He rolled off the curb and fell out of his wheelchair, and I can't lift him up."

Now sobbing, the boy asked the stunned executive, "Would you please help me get him back into his wheelchair? He's hurt and he's too heavy for me."

Moved beyond words, the driver tried to swallow the rapidly swelling lump in his throat. He hurriedly lifted the handicapped boy back into the wheelchair, then took out his fancy handkerchief and dabbed at the fresh scrapes and cuts. A quick look told him everything was going to be OK.

"Thank you, and may God bless you," the grateful child told the stranger.

Too shaken up for words, the man simply watched the little boy push his wheelchair-bound brother down the sidewalk toward their home.

It was a long, slow walk back to the Jaguar. The damage was very noticeable, but the driver never repaired the dented side door. He knew he needed to keep the dent there so he'd never forget its message: don't go through life so fast that someone has to throw a brick at you to get your attention.

Thinking about what our metapatterns are and getting into the habit of using them to our advantage to achieve greater self-confidence may take some effort, but it's effort that will more than pay off in the long run.

Assignments:
Putting Self-Confidence to Work

1. Identify the five metapatterns you display and evaluate them to see how many support the goals and outcomes you identified earlier.

2. Think of your values and goals and try to come up with three new or modified outcomes that would fit nicely into the metapatterns you already possess.

3. Think about altering your metapatterns to more successfully achieve your self-confidence goals. Is it possible to do that? What specifically would you need to do?

Seven

Using Optimism to Build Self-Confidence

A major part of self-confidence depends on how optimistic you are. There are several researchers who have done exhaustive study on optimism, including Mihaly Csikszentmihalyi (pronounced "mi-hi cheek-sent-me-hi") and Martin Seligman, the father of a very interesting concept: learned helplessness. Csikszentmihalyi is a professor of psychology at Claremont University in California, and Seligman is a professor of psychology at the University of Pennsylvania.

Csikszentmihalyi observed that when people restrain themselves out of fear, their lives are by necessity diminished. But his theories have dramatically gone beyond fear. In his book *Flow: The Psychology of Optimal Experience*, he discussed his research into the mental state of complete concentration and absorption when subjects are doing a highly desirable activity. In this state, they are so involved in the activity that nothing else seems to matter. Csikszentmihalyii calls it "the state of intrinsic motivation," or *flow*. Flow is very close to the feeling often described as "being in a zone" or "in a groove." This is a feeling everyone gets at some point, and it is characterized by great absorption, engagement, fulfillment as well as skill.

In one magazine interview, Csikszentmihalyi described flow as being completely involved in an activity for its own sake. Anxiety totally falls away. Time flies. Every action, movement, and thought follows from the previous one, like playing jazz. Your whole being is involved in using your skills to your utmost ability.

The great tennis player Pete Sampras displayed flow in a semi-final match at the U.S. Open, a year before he retired. He was in a heated competition against the great Spanish player Àlex Corretja. In a tiebreaker in the second set, it became very apparent that Sampras was very sick. At one point, he threw up on court against the back wall. There was no way he could finish the match. The whole crowd thought that he would default, giving his opponent a window to his first championship. But like all great champions, Sampras rallied back and won the tiebreaker. He then eked out a third-set victory, opening the way to the finals match. This dramatically illustrates Csikszentmihalyi's concept of flow. If Sampras had not been in a perfect state of flow, he would have felt the pain and nausea, the debilitating effects of headache and fever, and would have easily defaulted the match.

Csikszentmihalyi called this flow state an *autotelic experience*, from the Greek *autos*, meaning *self*, and *telos, end* or *goal*: it is something one does for the experience of doing it. To achieve a flow state, a balance must be struck between the challenge of the task and the skill of the performer. If the task is too easy or difficult, flow can't occur. Both skill level and challenge level must be both matched and high. If the skill and challenge are low and matched, then there is apathy. If I play tennis against a beginner, my skill level is high, but the challenge level is low. So there is no flow state. But if I play tennis against twenty-year-old touring pros with my sixty-something body, my skill level is too low and the challenge level is too great. I could never reach flow, because skill and challenge must be both matched and high.

Say you're a salesperson who's been working on a project for months. The prospect suddenly says yes. As you do the paperwork, a flow state occurs. That last interview could be ten minutes or three hours long—both would feel the same to you; you are in flow. In a golf match, you hit a drive off the tee farther than you have ever hit. It sails 320 yards. Then you nail your fairway shot to the middle of the green. You sink a one putt, for a birdie. You have achieved a flow state. The hole took fifteen minutes, but felt like one. This is flow.

Michael Jordan was about to shoot a three-pointer in game seven against the Utah Jazz. It was the NBA finals, and if Jordan could sink the shot with three seconds left, his Chicago Bulls would win another championship. The problem was that Jordan was sick that day, throwing up during halftime. He didn't even play much in the second half. But for that one critical shot, he was in a flow state.

Flow is a critical concept in self-confidence. If your skill level is much greater than the challenge, you will be self-confident but bored. If the challenge is much greater than your skill, your self-confidence will dissipate because you will feel tremendous anxiety.

A good example of this is giving a speech. You know your material and have done it in front of small groups of fifteen to twenty. Your skill level is high, but the challenge is low, so there is no flow. But when you speak in front of 2000 people, not only do you have to know the material, you have to entertain them to keep their attention. A greater skill level is demanded because the challenge is so high. If you don't possess enough skill to be brilliant in front of 2000 people instead of just fifteen, flow will be replaced by stress and anxiety.

It is not enough to push yourself to be confident at an activity; you must also have the skill level to match. So you would practice the speech many times, work on putting the right stories and humor in the right places. You would deliver it to large groups before your keynote to 2000 people. With every practice session, your confidence would increase. Your chance of achieving flow would be much greater.

One other research finding from Csikszentmihalyi is *intrinsic motivation*. He found that intrinsically motivated people were more likely to be goal-oriented and directed. These are precisely the kinds of people who enjoy challenges leading to an increase in overall happiness. Csikszentmihalyi noted that intrinsic motivation is a very powerful trait. It can optimize and enhance positive experience, feelings, and overall well-being just as a result of being challenged. This means that you should challenge yourself constantly. Challenge yourself in sports, your job, family, and every other area of your life. People with low self-confidence tend to avoid situations in which they can't perform well. They employ avoidance behaviors like saying, "I'm too tired," "I don't want to do it because I'm not that good," or even "I don't have time." But the research on intrinsic motivation suggests that trying new things in itself, whether you perform well or not, will increase your feeling of well-being and self-confidence.

One of the most interesting areas in developing optimism, self-esteem, and self-confidence is Seligman's concept of *learned helplessness*. This is very easy to understand. Once we fail at an activity, we often learn to avoid that same action in the future, because we have learned to never succeed at it.

Famed fashion designer Coco Chanel once said, "Success is most often achieved by those who don't know that failure is inevitable."

I am a research psychologist. I love to discuss the actual experiments used to reach conclusions like learned helplessness. In one experiment, a control group of dogs were put in harnesses for a period of time and released. In groups 2 and 3, they were put in yoked pairs. A dog in group 2 would be intentionally subjected to painful electric shocks, but the dog could end the shocks by pressing a lever. The group 3 dog was wired in series with the group 2 dog, receiving electrical shocks of identical intensity and duration. But the group 3 dog lever did not stop the electric shocks, no matter how many times it was pushed. To the group 3 dog, it seemed that the shocks ended at random, because it was his paired dog from group 2 that caused the pain to stop. The group 1 and group 2 dogs quickly recovered from the experience, but the group 3 dogs learned to be helpless. They also showed symptoms similar to chronic clinical depression.

In another experiment, Seligman and an associate, used three groups of dogs in a shuttle-box apparatus, in which the dogs could escape electric shocks by jumping over a low partition. The group 3 dogs, who had previously learned that nothing they did had any impact on the shocks, just lay down passively and whined. Even though all they had to do was jump over a partition, they didn't even try. The researchers call this *retardation of learning*, in which a learner doesn't try and just gives up.

One of the most interesting aspects of these experiments was what happened next with the group 3 dogs. The researchers would verbally encourage them, and even hold a treat as an incentive on the other side, to encourage them to jump the partition. But the dogs would just lie there, unresponsive to any threat or reward. The researchers actually had to pick the helpless dog up, move its legs, and lift it over the partition, teaching it how to escape the shock. The biggest surprise was that they had to do this twice before the dog learned it could escape the shocks.

These findings should not be entirely surprising to you. I'm sure you've been to a zoo or a circus. The elephants are tethered with a very light rope to a stake; they could easily escape. But obviously that is not the first time the elephant has been tethered. As a baby, it was chained to a metal stake from which it could not break free. No matter what the baby did, escape was futile. Gradually the elephant learned that anything around its leg, fastened to any structure, was also inescapable. This is learned helplessness.

In another experiment, this one with babies, a sensory pillow was used that could control the rotation of a mobile above the crib. If the baby moved its head to one side, the mobile would rotate, while movement to the other side would stop the mobile. Another group of babies was put into cribs that also had mobiles above their heads, but with no sensory pillows. Both sets of babies were later given sensory pillows that had full control over the rotation of the mobiles. Only those who had learned to control the mobile previously attempted to use it to control the mobile again. Obviously the first group of babies learned to control the mobile, while the second group of babies learned to be helpless in controlling it.

Several of my friends are ex–U.S. Navy SEALs. The SEALs' Basic Underwater Demolition School, or BUDS, is dramatic, excruciating, and more challenging than any other that is offered by the military. Not only are the SEALs subjected to ice-cold water for hours at a time, they are given one or two hours of sleep per night for weeks on end. Much of this is an attempt to weed out the less dedicated recruits. The trainers use one concept to teach the BUDS candidates how to escape from learned helplessness. (Of course the Navy doesn't call it that; they call it *unfairness*.) While the candidates are out on evening exercises, trainers will go in the barracks and take sheets off a couple of the beds. After eighteen hours of training, the candidates are so exhausted they can barely walk. As they enter the barracks, an inspection is announced, with the trainers looking for inconsistencies. Of course the trainers target the beds without sheets and punish the candidates who are not in compliance. While this is totally unfair and reprehensible to you and me, it teaches the candidates that unfairness will occur and needs to be overcome. "Guilty" candidates will accept their fate and spend the rest of the night without sleep as punishment. But the real lesson is to move on and succeed, even in the face of unfairness or learned helplessness.

This research is very important in showing you how to develop your own self-confidence with new activities. If you have failed at something in the past, you may have learned that it's futile to attempt it again in the future. As I mentioned earlier, I was cut by my junior-varsity basketball coach at sixteen years old. Unlike some superstars like Michael Jordan, who was also cut from his high-school basketball team, I never played competitive basketball again. I rationalized that I liked tennis, baseball, football, and golf a lot more. I'm not saying that coaches shouldn't cut weaker players, but we all should be aware of our tendency to give up and learn to be helpless. Just because you failed at something before doesn't mean you can't learn to do it effectively in the future.

Here are some people you have heard of who have overcome learned helplessness.

Walt Disney was fired from his job at a newspaper for "lacking ideas." He also had several bankruptcies and was turned down by over a hundred banks before he was able to develop Disneyland.

Fred Astaire kept a memo over his fireplace from an MGM testing director after his first screen test that said, "Can't act. Slightly bald. Can dance a little."

Vince Lombardi was told by an expert that he "possesses minimal football knowledge. Lacks motivation."

Bill Birdseye invented frozen foods. He discovered the secret of flash-freezing, which turned out to create an entire industry. This only happened after he went bankrupt seven times.

Bob Parsons, founder and CEO of the domain-registering site GoDaddy.com, overcame a lot in pursuit of his dream. He definitely was not an overnight success and experienced a lot of failure on the way. But he kept his vision in his mind at all times and said, "I spent very little time looking back or feeling sorry for myself." Another awesome quote from Parsons is, "Quitting is easy. The easiest thing to do in the world is to quit and give up on your dreams (and quite frankly, that's what all the nonrisk takers want you to do)."

Ludwig van Beethoven's teacher told him he was a hopeless composer.

Colonel Harlan Sanders, creator of Kentucky Fried Chicken, was rejected by over a thousand restaurants for more than a year while he lived in his car trying to sell his chicken recipe.

As I mentioned before, it's very difficult to adapt and make changes in your own personality. We can all learn and grow, but changing who we are, our core personality, is nearly impossible. You're probably thinking right now, "Why even read about self-confidence if I can't change?" But you can learn to be more self-confident. The difficulty is in the follow-up and the discipline to execute what you know.

The Resource Circle

A technique for dealing with learned helplessness and anxiety involves using a resource circle. Simply concentrate on a time or an event in which you were completely successful. The event could be winning a sporting contest, or giving a brilliant speech, or receiving an award. In your mind, draw an imaginary circle on the floor or ground next to you. Now try to access that past event. Try to see it. Try to hear the sounds around you as if you were there, and try to invoke the feelings you experienced when the event originally happened.

When you believe you are as close as possible to reliving the event, take a step into that imaginary circle. Then step out and repeat the exercise, recalling the event as it sounded, looked, and felt at the time. Now do it again without recalling the three senses. Just step right into the circle. You should be able to immediately access that same winning feeling just by stepping into the circle.

The great thing about practicing a resource circle is that in time, you will be able to access the winning feeling without doing any physical activity. Much as a crying baby is at first comforted in the arms of her mother. In time the baby just seeing Mom enter the room will produce the same calm. I recently spoke to a man who told me he felt horrible about being overweight, but his patience and self-confidence had come to an end. He was very stressed. He remembered the resource circle technique, mentally drew his circle on the ground, and stepped into it. Not only did his SUDS level go down to a peak performing level, he was able to reach inside himself and pull out strength he didn't know he had. He reached his weight-loss goal by controlling his anxiety.

Like this man, the most powerful coaches, businesspeople, athletes, professionals, and scientists are those who, on cue and largely unconsciously, put themselves into a powerful resource state by giving themselves certain signals. Many are able to do this in spite of horrible things that occur in their lives, whether it's ill health, financial breakdown, family problems, or other tragedies. They can keep themselves in a successful resource state by triggering powerful mechanisms in their minds.

Often before a football game, NFL players will pound each other on the shoulder pads. I thought this was a way to check the pads until I learned about resource circles. The players used the pounding almost as a way to motivate themselves and access pasts memories of wins. In this way, the players are able to increase the performance necessary to play at their best. But the fastest way they get motivated is by chanting in circles before a game. New Orleans Saints quarterback Drew Brees is one of the only quarterbacks who leads his team into a chant. It whips the team up so fast and so well that they are one of the fastest teams out of the starting block in the NFL.

You can use resource states to create your own self-confidence just as NFL players do. One that I used as a pro tennis player was the way I bounced the ball before a serve. I would bounce it exactly twice before a first serve and once before a second serve. You might think this is superstition, but I could put myself into a confident state just with this simple act.

Pro tennis player Rafael Nadal uses his own resource state. He tucks his hair behind both ears before receiving a serve. Superstition or resource state? A TV beer commercial once said, "It's only superstition if it doesn't work."

Attachment

One additional technique you can use to control anxiety is called *attachment*. Many athletes with performance anxiety use this to compete at their best. For example, before beginning a race, a sprinter will put her hands on her hips to access past relaxation or a past success before kneeling down to the starting blocks. A 400-meter dash is an enormously stressful endeavor. Many racers lose before they start, with a huge expenditure of anxiety in the minutes leading up to the race. But when an athlete can put her hands on her hips and calm herself down, she can gain control and put herself in a position to win. Some players will put their glasses on a certain way, or wear a certain watch or a special pair of socks. Roger Federer often wears the same (hopefully washed) shirt during his matches that he has worn during previous wins in a tournament. Often commentators talk about superstition. Possibly so. But if the player can access the same mental edge possessed during the last win, they have access a resource state.

Eight

Coping with Stress

In 1962, John F. Kennedy's assassination shocked the United States. A twenty-seven-year-old Army captain led the funeral procession transporting his body as a mourning nation grieved the loss. One week later, that same twenty-seven-year-old captain died of a massive heart attack.

A seventy-five-year-old man bet $2 on a long shot at the racetrack. When his horse won, he became ecstatic at the prospect of winning $1,600. He was so overwhelmed that just as he arrived at the window to collect his winnings, he collapsed and died.

Of these two victims, one was young; one was old. One died during a period of national grief, the other while feeling overwhelming joy. Yet they shared a common denominator: both experienced significant stress just prior to their death.

Odd as it may seem, all change, negative or positive, causes stress. The more unexpected the change, the greater the likelihood that stress will affect us. Sometimes this stress is mental, sometimes it is physical, sometimes it is spiritual. Most significant of all, many medical researchers believe that 70 percent of all medical problems are stress-related, yet only 2 percent of patients tell their physicians about the problems causing their stress.

Stress and Change

Stress not only accompanies every major life change from growing up to moving to a new community to aging, it also accompanies the changes that occur as we embark on a self-confidence program. This applies to any change, whether it involves losing weight, increasing wealth, or altering bad habits. This stress often diminishes our commitment, causing us to lose the motivation necessary to continue being self-confident. Ironically, the more successful you are at bringing confidence into your life, the more change you will experience. Conversely, stress is the enemy of self-confidence. The more you let stress into your life, the more you will struggle with self-esteem and self-confidence.

A life-insurance agent friend of mine doubled his income in 1984. It shot up so fast that he employed ten new administrative people to support him. He was able to spend more time with his family and experienced great pride in his achievement. Yet in November of that year, he contracted mononucleosis. He was bedridden for three months, and his business was soon near bankruptcy. Nearly a year later his wife left him, taking their three-year-old son. Stress was as much a factor in his setbacks as was his illness. His life had changed too quickly for both himself and his spouse.

In the short term, many causes of stress seem obvious. A prospect you are close to closing won't return your phone calls. A customer won't return the necessary paperwork after you have spent many months working with him. Perhaps you have office employees who move so slowly that they seem more like monolithic structures than alert human beings.

Our response to stress is fairly predictable. During stressful situations, we go through four stages of behavior: alarm, resistance, adaptation, and fatigue. Say a client of many years is approached by a competitor, and ultimately becomes convinced that the product you've sold him is obsolete and a bad investment. When you discover the transgression, you experience shock and alarm. How could this happen? How could your customer be so stupid as to listen to other people?

The next stage you experience is resistance. You may contemplate bombing your competitor's building or at least slicing his tires. You may walk up and down the hallways of your office complaining to everyone you see. You may feel yourself tensing more and more as you talk about your situation. After writing letters to well-chosen recipients, you decide the best thing to do is to call the client and explain to him how he was wronged.

Then you begin to adapt. You reason that it might be more work to pursue your former client than it is worth. You may even contemplate ways of preventing the problem in the future.

The final stage is fatigue. Even though you learned of the replacement only a few hours ago, your whole body feels as if a twenty-ton truck has run over it. Every muscle aches, and you're mentally exhausted and emotionally spent.

This example shows that the more time you spend resisting the stressful situation, the more fatigued you will be in the end. Likewise, the more strenuously you resist, the more fatigued you will be. If you've ever arm-wrestled, you know that each competitor tries to pin the other's hand and arm onto the table, and that each experiences one common result: exhaustion after the match.

In the late 1970s in Linz, Austria, I competed in a tennis tournament against an Austrian hometown champion. "Boris" was favored to win the tournament. In fact, the tournament director tried to ensure his win by entering him in the semifinals without competing in the preliminary rounds, like the rest of us. (It was common in those days for a celebrity to receive appearance fees under the table to entice him to show up. This appearance stipend was often more than the winner's purse.)

Boris won the first set. I was ahead five to three in the second set when Boris tossed the ball up to serve. But instead of serving the ball to me, he served his racket. He threw his tennis racket across the net, and it went whizzing over my head.

My alarm stage set in. I felt shocked that this could actually happen. I then resisted. I ran over to the chair umpire and demanded that Boris be ejected from the match. But the tournament directors weren't about to expel an investment property as valuable as their champion. I then adapted by realizing my efforts at retribution were useless. I walked back onto the tennis court and stood ready to play, but I felt exhausted, as though I had already played a five-set match. I had spent so much energy resisting the situation that I fatigued myself, and I was unable to play effectively. Boris went on to win the second set seven to five and take the match.

There are two distinctive types of stress. *Cannon stress* is named for the esteemed physiologist Walter Cannon, and *Selye stress* is named after the great Canadian endocrinologist Hans Selye. Both types work on the presumption of a weak link. Every one of us has a weak link physically or mentally. This weakness is the first part to break, and because of this, no two people will react to stress alike. Some may have heart attacks, while others, like me, lie awake with insomnia night after night during high-stress periods.

Cannon Stress

Cannon stress, also known as the fight-or-flight response, is based on a physiological reaction to stress. This response is useful during periods of physical threat. If you are a caveman, and attacked by a saber-toothed tiger, for example, Cannon stress will help you climb a tree faster than a cat.

During periods of physical threat, Cannon stress saves lives, but except for these unusual examples, it also takes lives. Physical symptoms of Cannon stress are:

1. **Muscle pain or illness.** Have you ever come home at the end of a bad day at the office feeling as if you've been run over by a tank? You may have been suffering from Cannon stress. Even if you didn't lift more than a pencil, the constant tensing and relaxing of muscles can leave you feeling as if you have run a marathon.

2. **Tension headaches.** Unlike migraines, this type of headache is caused by the tensing of cranial muscles. Often aspirin can help relieve this pain, although relaxation techniques are more effective in the long run.

3. **Irritable stomach.** Because the stomach muscles are also in tension, digestion continues in the form of acid release. The acid causes ulcerations in the stomach lining.

4. **High blood pressure.** The automatic tightening of muscles even affects the capillaries. Blood pressure is increased because

the blood is being redirected away from the extremities and toward the torso, putting pressure on the heart.

Some of the psychological symptoms of Cannon stress include:

1. **Intractable fatigue.** This is a condition in which you are actually too tired to sleep. After I have traveled through a number of time zones, I sometimes find my exhaustion is so great that I am actually unable to fall asleep.

2. **Insomnia.** Because the muscles in the body are kept in such a state of tension, you can't relax enough to fall asleep. Insomniacs often report being caught in a Catch-22 cycle of stress. They become so afraid of not sleeping at night that their anxiety levels soar, causing even more severe insomnia. You may experience this during periods of pressure at work or at home.

3. **High irritability levels.** Bobby Knight, ex–basketball coach for the Indiana Hoosiers, once threw a chair onto the court during a game because of his high irritability level due to tension. His temper got him into more trouble later, when he was accused of choking a player for being disrespectful. He was fired for violating the zero-tolerance policy the athletic director had initiated to curb his violent outbursts.

4. **Lack of concentration.** If you have ever flown, you have undoubtedly sat for long periods of time in an airport. Did you try to read or concentrate? During this high-stress time of waiting for a flight, it becomes difficult to concentrate or follow through on a thought. Instead you are paying attention to flight announcements and watching your belongings.

5. **Acute anxiety.** The psychological discomfort caused by stress stirs up apprehension and anxiety, occasionally to the point of fear.

Selye Stress

Selye stress works in a different way. Also reacting to perceived change, it causes problems with other systems in the body. Selye stress impact small muscles in the cardio-vascular system and even in skeletal muscles. It constricts the veins and blood vessels much as water pressure increases in a hose that is squeezed. When small muscles are squeezed in the digestive system, you may experience abdominal pain. Selye stress symptoms include:

1. **Migraine headaches.** These headaches cause more pain than simple headaches; it often feels as though pain is wrapped around the head or centered unilaterally in one area. Such headaches can result in flulike symptoms. Once they begin, it becomes difficult to break the cycle of pain.

2. **Rashes or skin eruptions.** You have undoubtedly seen people red-faced when upset. Others actually break out into a facial rash during stress. I worked with one person whose face turned red when she was stressed. I usually knew how much stress she was under just by looking at her blotchy skin.

3. **High vulnerability to illness.** Selye stress lowers the body's natural resistance to illness. If you have had the flu or a cold more than once this past year, you may be suffering from this kind of stress.

4. **Heart disease.** This is often due to coronary artery obstructions, which damage the heart itself. The arteries need to be elastic to allow blood to ebb and flow. Selye stress literally causes these arteries to narrow, making them susceptible to stricture and blockages. Arteriosclerosis is a hardening of the arteries made worse by stress. A majority of heart attacks occur between 8:00 and 9:00 a.m. on Mon-

day mornings. Apparently job stress is a great contributor to heart attacks.

5. **Cancer.** I never understood the true magnitude of how stress can affect cancer until I watched what happened to my mother. In 1979, even though she had never smoked a single cigarette in her life, she had a lung removed because of cancer. In February 1987, she collapsed in her home, paralyzed with a malignant brain tumor. Fortunately, her neurosurgeon was able to remove all of the cancerous tissue. After the operation he said that the cancer, latent for twelve years, had been activated by stress.

One theory is that cancer develops because stress fatigues the body's resistance level, making us more susceptible to cancer attacks. Another theory is that constant stress diminishes our normal resistance to the disease.

6. **Grey hair.** Even if you've been coloring your hair for years, you may be surprised to learn that the pigment of hair, called melanin, is destroyed during stress, leaving hair a premature grey.

7. **Male pattern baldness.** Baldness is obviously hereditary, but it can be accelerated during periods of high stress. The smooth scalp muscles may constrict the hair follicles, causing the hair shafts to fall out more quickly.

The psychological symptoms of Selye stress include:

1. **Depression.** Defined psychologically as loss, depression can trigger periods of hopelessness and helplessness. Serious depression can lead to suicidal thoughts. Over 70 percent of the adult population in America report serious depression at least once a year. The highest number of suicides in our society

occur between the ages of seventeen and twenty-five years old, ages of radical physical and emotional change. A loss could be a loss of a job losing a paycheck, divorce which is a loss of family, or even a tennis match. When I was on the pro tennis tour, players often said that the depression of losing a match was more emotionally intense than the joy of winning a match.

2. **Psychosis.** Psychosis is medically defined as a symptom or feature of mental illness typically characterized by radical changes in personality, impaired functioning, and a distorted or nonexistent sense of objective reality. Many psychologists believe that all of us possess latent psychotic tendencies. The line between normality and abnormality is a thin one. Stress-related pressures can push us across that line, causing ordinarily normal people to exhibit very unpredictable and unstable behavior.

Type A and Type B

Your personality type also contributes greatly to your stress level. Consider these questions: Does your behavior help you or hinder you in your efforts to achieve your goals? Do you roll with the punches or make things worse for yourself? Take this short test to determine your personality type. If you answer yes to ten or more of these questions, consider yourself a Type A personality. If you answer yes to fewer than ten of these questions, breathe a sigh of relief and consider yourself a Type B personality.

1. Do you finish others' sentences before they do?
2. Do you move, walk, or eat quickly?
3. Do you prefer a summary instead of skimming or scanning a complete article?

4. Do you become upset in slow lines of traffic?

5. Do you generally feel impatient?

6. Do you find yourself uninterested in or unaware of details?

7. Do you try to do two or more things at once?

8. Do you feel guilty if you relax or take a vacation?

9. Do you link your worth to quantitative tangibles like income, company growth, or number of employees?

10. Do you try to schedule more and more activities into less and less time?

11. Do you think about other things while talking to someone?

12. Do you exhibit nervous gestures like drumming your fingers or tapping your pen?

13. Do you continue to take on more and more responsibility?

14. Do you accentuate key words in an ordinary conversation when there is no reason to do so?

15. Do you work fast, even though deadlines are not pressing?

So how did you score? Ten or more? Then you are probably a type A person.

Type A Personalities

A textbook example of a Type A person is Barry, a successful, hard-working salesman. Barry likes his work very much. Barry is so proud of his sales achievements that he keeps constant reminders of his production on his desk. He is continually trying to increase his sales volume by working harder and harder, and he spends increasing hours in the office. As if that weren't enough, he uses a stopwatch to track production and often yells to his secretary, "We have three minutes left to complete this project." He also finds that his secretaries don't last very long. But when one leaves, Barry says, "I didn't really like her anyway."

Barry has trouble coping with traffic jams. He can't muster enough patience to wait in lines, even in fast-food restaurants. He rarely has time to attend family gatherings. He tries to motivate newcomers in his company by appealing to their great desire to achieve. He makes every effort to set a good example by never complaining to his colleagues, but in private he will unload his gripes to his wife about how a customer or business associate has upset him. He admits feeling stressed, especially about things he can't change.

Recently Barry visited a doctor who said his blood pressure and cholesterol count were too high. The doctor recommended that he watch his diet and learn to relax. It was easy for Barry to decrease his cholesterol level by cutting down on butter and eggs and other dairy products, but try to relax? Fat chance. To do nothing, or to be engaged in what he considers "nonproductive leisure," would be too uncomfortable to him. Barry has begun jogging to keep his heart going, but he's unaware that his arteries are clogged from the long-term effects of cholesterol and the chronic bombardment of hormonal secretions released by his constant anxiety.

Barry's chances of leading a normal life and reaching a ripe old age are practically nil, because Type A people like Barry run a higher risk of heart attack than Type B people. In fact, Type As are twice as likely to contract heart disease. In addition to the higher levels of both anxiety and depression they feel.

In his 1981 book *Type A Behavior and Your Heart*, cardiologist Meyer Friedman said that 20 percent of stressed patients contracted 80 percent of all cases of heart disease. He also determined that these individuals had a 70 percent greater chance of contracting heart disease than other patients. In short, these people had a greater tendency to feel stress and suffer psychological and physical pain from that stress. Their personality characteristics were much more likely to decrease their life expectancies.

Type B Personalities

Type B people react much differently than Type As. They are more relaxed but still highly productive people, who have profitable, long-lasting careers. Type B individuals examine their own behavior often to determine when and how they can change. They are sensitive to the needs of people around them. They are also more open and friendly and often more cooperative than Type As. They are not as time-conscious, yet they seem to be aware of the correct time. In short, they handle stress well and yet manage to get a lot done. Unfortunately, they often seem to be in short supply.

The Subjective Unit of Discomfort Scale

Now on to the good part: how to deal with stress. It is practically impossible to totally eradicate it, but you can learn to cope so well that you can cause your performance to improve rather than deteriorate, even under the most stressful conditions. And coping with stress effectively will help you increase your self-confidence.

Managing stress begins with knowing how much stress you have. Look at the Subjective Unit of Discomfort Scale, or SUDS, on the next page to help you measure your physical and psychological response to stressful situations. They are measured in increments from 0 to 100. Each of these subjective units (0, 5, 10, 15, 20, 30, and so on) also corresponds to symptoms you may have as a result of stressful situations.

Subjective Unit of Discomfort Scale SUDS

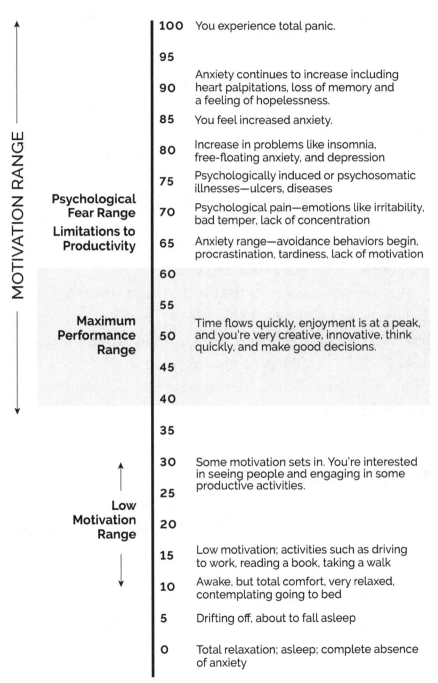

MOTIVATION RANGE

	100	You experience total panic.
	95	
	90	Anxiety continues to increase including heart palpitations, loss of memory and a feeling of hopelessness.
	85	You feel increased anxiety.
	80	Increase in problems like insomnia, free-floating anxiety, and depression
	75	Psychologically induced or psychosomatic illnesses—ulcers, diseases
Psychological Fear Range	**70**	Psychological pain—emotions like irritability, bad temper, lack of concentration
Limitations to Productivity	**65**	Anxiety range—avoidance behaviors begin, procrastination, tardiness, lack of motivation
	60	
	55	
Maximum Performance Range	**50**	Time flows quickly, enjoyment is at a peak, and you're very creative, innovative, think quickly, and make good decisions.
	45	
	40	
	35	
	30	Some motivation sets in. You're interested in seeing people and engaging in some productive activities.
	25	
Low Motivation Range	**20**	
	15	Low motivation; activities such as driving to work, reading a book, taking a walk
	10	Awake, but total comfort, very relaxed, contemplating going to bed
	5	Drifting off, about to fall asleep
	0	Total relaxation; asleep; complete absence of anxiety

A low-stress situation, such as having a relaxing drink in front of the fireplace, measures 0. High-stress situations measure 100, such as following a group of Hell's Angels on the freeway with your car horn stuck.

What levels of stress on this scale do you experience during an average day? What are your lowest and highest levels? If your SUDS level is generally higher than 45, it's too high, and you may suffer symptoms of burnout. If your SUDS level drops below 30, it's too low, and you may experience "rustout."

The following chart will give you a good idea of the symptoms you may experience. If you can keep yourself between 30 and 45, you will stay in a peak performance range. Everything will flow, you'll lose track of time, and you'll do your best work.

When I play tennis, my SUDS level is always between 30 and 45, and two hours feel like five minutes. When I'm prospecting for new business, I enter this flow range when I start to enjoy the telephone calls. But if I let my discomfort rise above 45, I will perform more poorly in selling situations. The same is true if I decrease my discomfort below 30.

Progressive Relaxation

One extremely effective technique for decreasing your SUDS manageable level is progressive relaxation. Nearly everybody who successfully copes with stress applies some form of relaxation technique. Many salespeople pay enormous amounts of money to be hooked up to a biofeedback machine in order to relax. The technique I'm about to explain serves equally well for relieving symptoms and producing more relaxation.

Make sure you are comfortably seated. Then tense and relax your muscles as you inhale and exhale, mentally moving through every general area of your body. Start with your ankles and feet, and slowly move all the way up to the muscles in your head. As you pause in each area, tense for a period of three seconds while you inhale and exhale, then relax the muscles and release.

After you've completed this step, imagine yourself at the top of a staircase with ten steps. Feel yourself inhaling and exhaling slowly with each step, as you start from step 1 and descend all the way down the staircase to step 10, becoming more relaxed with every step. When you get to the bottom of the staircase, imagine yourself beneath an oak tree in a grassy meadow. Hear the birds chirping in the trees and the wind blowing softly through the leaves. Leave yourself under the tree for about ten minutes. This exercise may be so relaxing that you could actually fall asleep for a short time. When you are really relaxed, you will experience a slight feeling of floating. Your muscles may even tingle.

To come out of this state, see yourself at the bottom of the staircase again, this time going up three steps. With every step up, take a breath in, and slowly let a breath out. With every breath, you will become more aware of the things around you. After the third step, open your eyes. You should be very alert, very aware, and very comfortable.

If you do this for the next seven days, you will be able to bring your body down to a fully relaxed, stress-free state. Many people who have used this technique for two weeks are able to simply picture the meadow and tree and feel more relaxed without having to mentally walk down the staircase.

Some of my clients will combine their resource state with the bottom of the staircase. They will touch themselves on the arm, for example, at the most relaxed moment. Then during a stressful situation, or when they feel anxiety, they will touch the same place on the arm, bringing back the same low-SUDS comfort they felt at the bottom of the staircase. This technique can be especially useful in meetings, or when you come face-to-face with a difficult coworker or customer.

The PQRS Technique

A second technique for dealing with the effects of stress is the PQRS technique. The initials stand for *prepare, question, relax,* and *solve.*

1. **Prepare.** Without question, being prepared for a stressful situation helps you cope with it. If you know you have a meeting tomorrow morning with a difficult prospect, get eight hours of sleep and eat a good breakfast beforehand. Also make sure you take a complex of B1, B3, B6, and B12 vitamins and decrease your intake of coffee, tea, or other stimulants.

2. **Question.** If we resist stress or stressful situations, we will feel more fatigued afterward. In other words, the effects of stress will be much more debilitating. So question your response. Is the situation really worth getting upset over? Is it something you want to make an issue of, knowing full well that the stress you receive from fighting it might not be worth the benefit?

3. **Relax.** Plan to spend five minutes out of every ninety simply sitting in your office, mentally walking yourself down the staircase and into the meadow and lying under that tree. If you do this, your

self-confidence will increase, because you will think more clearly and concisely.

4. **Solve.** It's not the elephants that get you; it's the mosquitoes. The little things that eat at us bit by bit, every day, eventually cause our anxiety balloons to burst. But if you engage in a problem-solving campaign to make sure the little things don't defeat you, you will be able to manage them with ease. Solve means to reach a solution to issues that might worry you. Even small problems and concerns can cascade into overwhelming problems. One of my colleagues procrastinated reprimanding a problem employee and just let it go. He didn't want to confront the staffer. The employee had other communication issues as well like being rude to other team members. But it wasn't until the employee yelled at a customer did the manager act. The problem employee could have been dealt with much earlier with a lot less drama if the manager had acted and solved the situation in the beginning.

Progressive Massage

A third technique for dealing with stress is progressive massage. The best place to apply it is at the base of the neck, the top of the shoulders, and where the spine meets the head. When you eliminate stress here, you relax and pave the way to feeling more self-confident about everything you do.

You might ask your spouse or a friend to give you a massage or a shoulder and neck rub. I recently saw a chiropractor for back pain. He specializes in deep-muscle massage. He mentioned that he often sees sedentary office workers with tight knots in their back and arms, all from stress. Kneading these knots out can be painful, depending on how much of the muscle is tied up.

Coping with Worry

What if a customer decides not to buy? What if you can't lose twenty pounds in time to fit into that dress? What if next month's sales are as bad as this month's? What if you fail to make the bonus you earned last year? What if? What if? What if?

Stress and worry go hand in hand. If you can control the latter, the former decreases as well.

A wise philosopher once said, "Worry is the interest paid on trouble that is not yet due." In spite of this, you spend too much time worrying. Some psychologists believe worry is a natural neurosis that indicates a lack of security, bred by childhood feelings of inadequacies. Other psychotherapists, such as Alan Loy McInnes, author of *Power Optimism*, believe we are victims of the media, who make money by whipping up our feelings of worry.

One thing is certain: worry paralyzes all of us, perhaps especially the best and the brightest. If you are serious about becoming more self-confident, you are a likely candidate for worry. After all, it is an indication that you are motivated, concerned, and serious about making changes in your life for the better.

In their book *Not to Worry*, authors Mary McClure Goulding and Robert L. Goulding argue that worrying is a waste of time, but they also believe that worriers are helped along in their destructive behavior by three types of people: rebels, reassurers, and caretakers.

Rebels are a worrier's worst nightmare. They are the types who try to give you something to really agonize about. They stay out late, refuse to call in, purposely make mistakes in financial records, drive recklessly, or refuse to get medical attention when you deem it necessary. When mom says to make sure to eat a good breakfast every morning while at college, the rebel instead drinks it, by downing a can of beer. When a man tells his wife that her driving scares him, she drives extrafast.

Reassurers perpetually try to cheer you up. They say things like, "Everything will work out, so don't worry." Or, "Your worries have never been proven out. You always figure something out." Reassurers seem like the reincarnation of mom. In fact, many worriers call their moms often to hear this kind of empty, but welcome, encouragement. Some reassurers even try to dispel the worry with well-thought-out facts. They say things like, "You've worried about this same issue for the last three months, and nothing has happened yet." But even this sort of discussion has little effect on the chronic worrier.

Caretakers spend much of their time taking care of the worrier's anxieties. They install extra locks on every door. They make phone calls confirming appointments or heading off potential fears. They try to gain control of situations in a world that can never be controlled.

The first step in coping with your worry is to figure out where you fit into this scheme. Are you primarily a rebel, a reassurer, or a caretaker? Then modify your behavior accordingly. If you're a reassurer, avoid asking the worrier to discuss her worries. You wouldn't ask a hypochondriac to talk about his medical maladies, so why do it with a worrier? Try to point your conversation away from areas that are likely to disturb them. Another great technique is to direct the conversation away from worry and into success. Most of us try to change the subject when our children harangue us to buy something, or to let them go out against our wishes, and the same technique works with worriers.

The second step in coping with worries is to have faith. Suffice it to say that when we are able to be thankful for our problems as well as our successes, worry ceases to hold much credibility.

Is it realistic to completely exist without worry? Only if you don't care. All of us worry from time to time, but often worry depends on how much control we allow events and experiences to have over us. Those with a high degree of self-confidence tend not to worry as much as those who have a lower level of confidence. Highly self-confident people tend to think of their circumstances as manageable. They believe they can work with any situation and create success out of it. Those with less self-confidence tend to think of circumstances as beyond their control. They are less likely to believe they can make lemonade out of lemons.

Alan Loy McInnes outlines five characteristics of people without worry that all of us can strive to emulate:

1. Nonworriers aren't often surprised by trouble. They are realists who understand that trouble is what builds us and that how we deal with it results in personal growth.

2. They have control over their future. They have the confidence that things happen because they choose to let them happen.

3. They allow for regular renewal. Their growth is so important to them that if they don't grow, they die emotionally.

4. They are cheerful even when they can't be happy. You have probably heard the phrase, "Fake it till you make it." This was obviously created for the optimists among us. They don't wear paste-on smiles, but they do realize that enthusiasm can improve a bad situation.

5. They accept what can't be changed. Optimistic, self-confident people constantly learn new ways to deal with their problems. They also are confident that their goals needn't change, just

their methods of achieving them. Worriers and pessimists are often so stubborn in their plans that they resist and rebel. They then complain about how unfair things are when their intransigence causes them to fail.

Worry is contagious, but not incurable. It is learned, not inherited. Granted, if you have spent a lifetime learning how to worry, it's difficult to learn to be optimistic. But if worry is interest paid on trouble that is not yet due, now's the time to close the account.

Coping with Lack of Time

Unfortunately, there's something more that causes us stress: a lack of time. It seems that no one has enough of it anymore. The man in this short story is typical of men and women both.

John, a successful salesman in his early forties, is trying to apply the self-confidence techniques he has learned. He is trying to stay in shape by riding the exercise bike for thirty minutes every morning. He watches his caloric input and decreases his carbohydrates. But in his work life, things are rough. Today alone, John needs to process the paperwork on five more sales by noon and has another ten issues to iron out with his home office. He is falling behind in his customer calls, and can't even get the standard paperwork done. His wife is losing patience with him, claiming he isn't the man she married. He hasn't spent more than ten minutes with his kids in the last week. All this, and he can't even claim he's making more money.

John feels more and more stressed as the week goes on. It doesn't make sense. He is becoming more confident and getting more done. He is more effective at work than even a month ago. He should be able to coast a little. But his work is more demanding than ever, and he's enjoying it less.

He rationalizes that he will eventually make more money—as if money will make up for the stress—but even that isn't happening yet.

If you are like most professionals, your company probably isn't considering hiring staff to support you. In fact, they are likely thinking of whom they can fire to increase return. Can they get another 2 percent output and increase their revenue?

There are only two ways to respond: You can do nothing and be whittled away, little by little, by stress. Or you can learn to cope with stress by using the techniques we have discussed. We all have the same amount of time; we just choose to prioritize it differently. Luckily, we can use these six techniques to deal with the pressure of not having enough time.

Six Techniques for Dealing with Time Crunch

As I mentioned before, stress is the enemy of self-confidence. The more stress, the less confidence. But most stress is self-inflicted. Here are six techniques you can use to avoid stress self-sabotage.

1. **Stop fighting self-created fires.** If you are spending more than 25 percent of your day fixing problems, you may be causing them in the first place. A few years ago, a client told me his business was hurting because he didn't have sufficient time to spend gaining new customers. I analyzed his day, hour by hour, and determined that he indeed wasn't spending enough time marketing. Instead

he was instead fixing computers, fighting overdue notices, and rectifying mistakes by his own staff. Surprised, I worked backwards and learned that he hired good people, but only gave them minimal training and then sent the new hires to the wolves. Training after the first day was conducted only after a mistake was made. The problem was, the same wolves kept coming back to bite him.

Poor training creates poor motivation, and poor motivation creates black holes of wasted money. The lesson is simple: when you hire someone new, take at least 25 percent more time to train them than you think is needed.

You can use this concept whether you're in business or not. After all, many of our fires are the result of waiting until the last minute to do what needs to be done. Use the techniques we have learned so far to start tasks earlier. For example, my wife adjusts all the clocks in our house ahead by fifteen minutes to make sure she is on time. In a way this is ridiculous—we all know the clocks are fast. But the results speak for themselves. We all pay attention to the fact that the clock is ticking, and we'd better be ready.

Also, try to fight fires only in the afternoons. This may not work for critical emergencies, but in general, you can train your staff to bring issues to you only during certain time windows of the day. The alternative is to fight fires all day long and lose control of your day as a result.

2. **Keep your short-, medium-, and long-term goals on your desk in plain view.** Short-term goals are for the near future, medium-term goals are for the next three to five years, and long-term goals are more than five years away.

Jack Welch, the famous General Electric CEO, once said, "Remember, if you aren't working daily toward your goals, you are helping someone else achieve theirs. Control your own destiny, or someone else will."

It is easy to fall into the trap of maintaining your business or your life instead of growing it, but maintaining the status quo today will mean deterioration tomorrow. Make time to build your business and your goals every day. After all, if you are trying to work on your golf swing, do you only practice it before a golf round? If you are trying to spend more time exercising, do you let two weeks go by since your last walk? Do you sell only when you are desperate and procrastinate making calls when business is good?

While it is often difficult to begin less appealing activities, try giving the most undesirable jobs the highest priority. Helen Gurley Brown, editor in chief of *Cosmopolitan* magazine, said she always did the most unpleasant things on her list first to get them out of the way.

If all this sounds trite and obvious, you're jaded. The winners in any industry, who are regularly in the top 5 percent, stick to their daily goals like glue. They review them in the morning before the day starts, and plan out the next day before the current one is done. They always have their goals in mind. They also hold planning sessions monthly, trying constantly to stay on track. This doesn't mean they never derail, but when they do take a detour, it's only a short distance back to the main track.

3. **Sharpen your axe.** Consider this story:

A lumberjack stayed home one day rather than going out with the other lumberjacks to cut wood. They ridiculed him for his absence and told him that he'd fall behind if he didn't come. The next day he

cut twice as much wood as all the others. When the other woodcutters
saw this, they asked what had made him so much more effective. The
lumberjack answered, "Yesterday I stayed home to sharpen my axe."

I spoke at a large convention a few years ago for the mortgage business. Sally Ride, the first female astronaut in space, was the keynote speaker. My presentation was in the afternoon, and I arrived an hour early that morning to get a good seat in the auditorium of 1500-plus seats. Out of the 3000 registered for the conference, 150 people showed up. What did Ms. Ride have to do to attract an audience? Catch a bullet in her teeth?

Compare that to the life-insurance industry's Million Dollar Round Table (MDRT) annual meeting. I spoke to 6000 at their June 1998 meeting. There were exactly 6000 seats in the auditorium. If you weren't there by 8:00 a.m. you didn't get in. No one was late. No one was in the foyer chatting or in their hotel enjoying a late breakfast. People came to get an edge, to get better. To sharpen their axes. By the way, just to be *invited* to the MDRT, your income for the preceding year had to be at least $150,000. Most in attendance made far more.

The difference between the mortgage and MDRT conference was the commitment and desire to gain and edge. The insurance agents were there to gain any insight that would help them. The mortgage attendees were they mainly as a break from their 8–5 job.

4. Remember that a messy desk is not the sign of a tidy mind. You should never waste time looking for items that should be at your fingertips. Keep essential items neatly organized. Only handle messages once. Read each email and immediately answer it, file it, forward it, or discard it. Do the same with your regular mail. That way you won't have to read it twice.

5. **Stop sitting at your sit-downs.** Have you ever noticed how much time is wasted in meetings you didn't want to attend in the first place? Start holding them standing up. Meetings stay focused and end quickly when people don't relax so much that they digress to other topics.

Another good idea is to schedule appointments and meetings at odd times. If you schedule a meeting for 10:00 a.m., most people will expect it to last until 11:00 a.m. If the appointment is at 10:20 or 10:17, the meeting will automatically carry the expectation of being short.

6. **Don't get trapped into the "hurry sickness."** Do you rush even when you don't have to? Do you become impatient in lines even on Sundays? Do your thoughts turn to work on your time off? If so, you are suffering from hurry sickness. Dr. James Dobson had a spot on his *Focus on the Family* radio show in which a prominent psychologist described this malady. He talked about a single-mindedness so intense that even time off becomes "time on." Be aware of whether this tendency lurks inside you. If it does, deliberately choose to behave differently.

It's abundantly obvious that stress can rob you of self-confidence, but it doesn't have to. You can employ stress-reduction techniques to get more enjoyment out of life. Use the techniques described in this chapter to control stress and worry and cope with time crunches. When you do, you will not only be happier, you'll also be healthier.

Assignments:
Putting Self-Confidence to Work

1. Evaluate your stress on a daily or even hourly basis by measuring your SUDS level at regular intervals. Use the techniques mentioned earlier to decrease your stress. One great reminder is to put a drop of fingernail polish on your watch. Whenever you look at the time, the polish will remind you to check your SUDS level. If it's too high, you can use these techniques to decrease your stress and discomfort.

2. Identify three situations that are causing you stress. You may be thinking that you don't feel all that stressed. It's sort of like the old saw about the frog: If you put a frog in boiling water, it will quickly jump out. But if you put the frog in cold water, and slowly heat it up, it will boil to death. You are that frog. You need to prevent stress from having an adverse effect on you even if you're not aware of it. Begin by applying the techniques of progressive relaxation, PQRS, progressive massage, the resource circle, and attachment. Feel free to overlap these techniques and use them together.

Nine

Raising Self-Confident Kids

One of the questions I get most is how to instill self-confidence in kids. Every parent knows that if you don't teach your kids, their friends will. A lot of research has also shown that the more self-confidence your kids can learn at an early age, the more equipped they will be to say no when they need to. Peers can usually get their friends to say yes. I always wanted my girls to be able to say no. But there is more to it. I want my kids to experience life and try new things instead of fearing the consequences.

The Age of Permissive Parents

Dr. Ruth Peters, a family therapist in Florida, and author of the book *It's Never Too Soon*, blames poor parenting for many of kids' self-confidence problems. Her notion is that parents have raised a generation of kids who have never had to take no for an answer and have never had to struggle. She believes parents have become too tolerant, allowing children to make decisions that parents ought to make for them. She also maintains that mothers and fathers in two-income families feel guilty about spending so much time away from home. As a result is, they feel unable to consistently apply stiff rules and regulations. What's more, they trade time with their kids for purchases in toy stores, handing out money in a guilt-ridden pseudogenerosity that only serves to teach their children that if they ask long enough, they can get anything they want.

The problem is, parents have taken the struggle away from their kids. It is like the butterfly struggling out of the cocoon: the fight is what strengthens the butterfly's wings. Most parents don't let their kids develop self-confidence because they don't allow their kids to strengthen their wings.

One typical mom in Dallas worries that her four-year-old daughter doesn't have a traditional two-parent family. Debbie works full-time and attends college in her spare moments. She is single, so Molly spends her day in child care, while Debbie worries that she may not be able to give Molly the material goods she deserves. Debbie tries to make up for her lack of time with Molly by giving her what she wants. When Molly demands cookies for breakfast, Debbie complies. When Molly screams and throws tantrums, Debbie acquiesces instead of sticking by her rules. She thinks it just isn't worth the fight. Yet Debbie is the first to say that it's important for Molly to learn she can't always get what she wants.

Make no mistake: being consistent in disciplining your children and teaching them self-confidence when they are young are two of the most important factors for raising happy, healthy, respectful, and responsible kids. When we try to give kids trouble-free lives, we take away not only the struggle but also the self-confidence they could learn by succeeding.

Although setting behavioral limits and rules may be somewhat arbitrary, barriers for kids are not unfairly stifling. In fact they are just the opposite. In a study done years ago, researchers found that kids stayed in the center of a play area that did not have a fence. When the play area was fenced in, kids would venture out to the perimeter. This study concluded that kids need boundaries to develop the self-confidence necessary to explore their surroundings.

Self-confidence builds in kids an understanding of themselves and a framework from which they can cope with life's difficulties, frustrations, and disappointments. Self-confidence also gives kids the tenacity and perseverance to focus on a task for as long as is necessary to complete it. In this way they learn and perfect their abilities to become adults who make achievement and growth a habit. They can't do this if Mom or Dad completes tasks for them, or buys whatever they want without having to earn it.

Unfortunately, like Debbie, most parents today are so overwhelmed by their work and family demands that they are exhausted at the very time they need to apply consistent lessons in self-confidence. As a result, they try to protect, prepare, and soothe their young instead of allowing them to suffer the consequences of their behavior. Consequently, kids are allowed to do what they want when they want it.

When children are able to take control, the results are predictable. According to a study done by Public Agenda, a New York public research organization, children under the age of twenty-one are increasingly lacking in morality and ethics. The study, funded by Ronald McDonald House Charities and the Advertising Council, asserts that the biggest problem of youth today is an absence of such basics as honesty, self-confidence, and a work ethic. Probably no generation has ever thought the current crop of kids was as respectful and ethical as they were at the same age, but this new research provides a look at the fire behind the smoke.

According to author Steve Farkas, 81 percent of adults believe parenting today is harder than ever, but 83 percent acknowledge that being a kid is also tougher. Surprisingly, the study showed, these adults don't believe time spent with kids is a factor in how moral and ethical they are. Nor do they think race, age, economic, or parental status are factors.

Many parents consider the threat of legal action to be important. Who hasn't heard reports of parents prosecuted under the statutes of child abuse for spanking their kids? My eight-year-old daughter once told me, just before she was disciplined for lying, that I wasn't allowed to spank her and that the police would arrest me if I did.

I just smiled and did the deed, but I couldn't help but wonder if she was right. Abuse is now defined as emotional trauma and threatening a child's welfare. But what child *doesn't* feel emotional trauma during punishment? This feeling of government intrusion has an enormous influence on parents' perceptions of how they should—and can—raise their kids. We aren't talking here about stories of NFL players taking a tree branch to their kids. We're talking about simple discipline.

Moving Children towards Self-Confidence

Moving children towards self-confidence begins by assessing their abilities, skills, and emotional capabilities. You wouldn't expect a two-year-old to spend the day cleaning the toy room, but you could ask him to help you pick up, at first by putting only a few toys away, then more the next time. At age ten, you might ask him to pick up his room and make his bed before school. Tough to enforce? Yes, if you try to initiate the task all at once. But if you have expected your child to clean his room daily, and have consistently enforced that request, it is as easy as making breakfast. Any chore done consistently is a good path to building self-confident kids.

In my household, daughters Catherine and Caroline were always responsible for cleaning up before they move on to play, but it took daily consistency on our part to enforce this. You can't enforce your rules once or twice a week and expect your child to be responsible for the rest of the month. One harried single mother recently told me that she is tired at the end of the day. The last thing she wants is to create conflict with her kids, especially when she hasn't seen them all day. She just wants to enjoy them. I asked, was she trying to be a parent, or was she using her kids for entertainment? She thought I was abrupt, but I made my point.

You don't need to feel that you can't enjoy time with your kids if you make rules and enforce them. A lot can be accomplished by the attitude you set. Yelling at your kids because they fail to clean a room in a timely manner will cause stress for everyone, but allowing your kids to do what they want will create more problems for them as adults. At the same time, yelling at your kids instead of encouraging them is an enemy of self-confidence. Kids don't need to be made to feel perfect, just accepted. They need to be able to hit standards within their reach, and then to be praised for their accomplishment.

Playing with your children, and joking as you all clean the room together, is the type of work/play kids love. When Catherine was ten, all she wanted to do was play chase in the house. I negotiated with her that I would play hide-and-seek three times, but after that she had to clean her room. She always wanted to play more.

Who cares if your kids receive a treat before they begin their chores? Lighten up. They are only kids. Make work fun for them, especially when you first set rules. Later they won't dread living by them.

The Importance of Praise

You can also move children towards self-confidence by praising them. Praise has been shown to be the most valuable currency in increasing business productivity. It ranks even higher than money in the minds of employees. It is even more effectively used in developing self-confident kids, both when they're small and when they're teens.

Praise works to build your child's self-esteem while encouraging the behavior you would like to see repeated. Praising your child is more fun than reprimanding, although both are necessary. If you are doing it right, you will praise substantially more than you correct. Think of your child's self-worth as a bank account. If you constantly make withdrawals with corrections and criticisms, the balance will be low. When it gets to zero, your child will act out with tantrums, yelling, aggression, and a myriad of other symptoms. But if your child's emotional bank account has frequent deposits of praise and acceptance and love, his sense of security will be strong, allowing him to stay confident in the tasks he attempts.

There is a place for punishment, of course. If your child were to run in the street chasing a ball, you would yell and scream instead of kindly asking that he not do it again. Such situations demand an immediate and strong response. Punishments work well, but they're also painful, to be reserved for only the most crucial situations.

At a mall recently, I followed a young mother with her ten-year-old son. He obviously didn't want to be there and kept drifting off behind her. Exasperated, she yelled at him to keep up by saying, "Why do I always have to ask you twice to do things? Why can't you be like your sister and just do the things I tell you to do?" Such harping causes a child not only to resent the parent but also to think that he can't succeed because he isn't good enough. That will kill self-confidence.

Parenting is 1 percent knowledge and 99 percent patience. After you have asked your child for the fifth time to clean her room and still doesn't do it, you may feel totally justified in yelling and screaming, but you would be totally wrong to do it. Your child needs you to build her self-esteem and self-worth so she can eventually build it herself. The way you discipline shows how much worth your kid holds in your eyes.

You may be thinking that your kids don't do anything worth praising. Don't wait for them to do something right! Catch them in the act of doing something *close* to being right and praise them for it.

Successive Approximation

Successive approximation focuses on praising children not when they do things right, but when they do them things better. It is praising kids when they are close to doing something you want. Not only is it easy to implement, it works with small children as well as teens. Instead of waiting for your kids to do something perfect, praise them just for starting a job. A kind word, a hand on the shoulder, a smile, and a hug, are all techniques you can use to praise your kids. Not only are these effective, they are the best ways to encourage your kids to do what you want.

I once asked my girls to take turns doing the dishes after dinner. The idea was to get them to alternate, one doing the dishes one week, and the other the next. The problem was, they often forgot. A gentle reminder usually did the trick, but a big gush of praise as they started toward the kitchen worked even better.

This technique works in stages. Once she knew what was expected of her, I praised eight-year-old Caroline for merely taking the dishes off the table. The next day, I praised her only when she scraped the food into the compacter. The following day, I praised her only when she reached the rinsing stage. The threshold for receiving praise was low at first; she gradually had to do more to get praise and approval. At the end of the week, she received praise only when she did a good job from start to finish.

The objective is to create an inner reward, a type of self-praise that is reflected later in life as self-esteem. I knew I wouldn't be able to be there to praise Caroline as an adult. It was important for her to know that if she took on a task, she would feel that just doing it right would increase her self-confidence.

Here is a list of phrases you can use to build self-confidence in your child:

You did a great job on that.
Tell me how you did so well.
I can see how hard you worked on this.
You must feel very proud.
I'd like to try that too.
I hope I can do as good a job as you.
You have put a lot of thought into this.

You can create more appropriate phrases than these, of course. The idea is to catch your children in the act of doing something right.

Using successive approximation will create in them a desire for completion and the tenacity to strive even when they feel like giving up.

The Importance of Touch

Researchers at the University of Minnesota discovered years ago that we can be persuaded not only by words but also by touch. The two together can be used to create a memory that will last a lifetime. To test the power of touch, two researchers left a quarter in a public phone booth. This was before the days of mobile phones, when the only way to make a call was to find a booth on a street corner. They would wait for someone to pick the quarter up from the ledge and walk out. Then one researcher would approach the individual and ask, "Did you find my quarter?" Only 23 percent of the culprits admitted taking the 25 cents.

On another occasion, a researcher touched a stranger on the arm below the elbow, asking the same question: "Did you find my quarter?" In this case, 83 percent of the phone-booth users returned the quarter. The researchers concluded that the participants were more persuaded to give the quarter back when touch was involved.

Other studies have shown that people remember ideas longer when they are touched as they are spoken to.

I tried this concept in a restaurant many years ago. After speaking to the National Restaurant Association, I asked one manager to let me train his servers to increase tips. He was thrilled that I would be willing to help, but he claimed that only great service could increase the size of tips. I told him that wasn't true. It was merely the *perception* of great service that would increase tips.

I taught his servers to touch the likely bill payer on the arm as they gave him the check. Then I taught them to say, "I have really enjoyed serving you. Please come again soon." Other servers were asked to say the words, "I have really enjoyed serving you. Please come again soon" but without the touch.

The servers using the words and the touch together increased tip amounts by 150 percent. Customers were also asked after their meal what they thought of their server. The ones who received the touch were significantly happier with their service than the customers who weren't touched.

This research speaks volumes about how you should praise your kids. If you would like your children to remember your praises longer and be more accepting of them, touch them as you tell them things you want them to retain. Authors Spencer Johnson and Ken Blanchard pioneered this concept in their book *The One Minute Manager.*

Three-Step Praise

What I call *three-step praise* works like this: First, praise your children in front of others. This will build them up in front of their friends as well as potentially causing their siblings to desire praise as well.

The next step is to praise your child specifically for the behavior you want to encourage. Say, "You did a great job raking the yard. And thanks so much for doing it on the first request." As you say this, touch your child on the arm or shoulder to reinforce the comment.

Lastly, tell your child how proud you are, and how well he is doing. He needs to associate approval with compliance with your rules and requests. When you praise him for a good job, he will make the same association when he needs to complete a project even when you aren't there to praise him. This is the beginning of self-confidence—developing their ability to accomplish.

When my daughter Catherine was ten years old, I asked her to take out the recyclable cans and papers whenever she saw them accumulate. The first day she ignored the job. The second day I reminded her. Later that day, she opened the door to look at the papers and cans. I saw her do it and praised her by saying, "Thanks, Catherine, for remembering to take out the recyclables," even though she hadn't so much as lifted one can. But she did grimace a "Sure" and took them out. I wouldn't have cared at that point if she had picked up a single can. I was only concerned with using successive approximation in order to praise her for *almost* doing what I wanted.

The next day I reminded her again, but I praised her only when she took a bottle out to the recycler. The following day, she totally forgot the chore. I didn't remind her, thinking she needed to remember it on her own.

The day after that, I asked her to come out to the garage, out of earshot from her friend, who was over for the day. I told her that she wasn't doing her chores and that I wanted her to do the job without my asking. She told me on the spot that she couldn't do it right then, and it had to wait until her friend left. I repeated my reprimand more assertively, but without yelling. I then touched her and said she was doing a great job with all her other chores. I told her how proud I was for the responsibility she was taking on, and how well she was handling it. Catherine smiled and said "Sure" again. But this time her smile was one of pride instead of inconvenience.

My daughter Caroline was a little more challenging. She would often run to Mom if she suspected that Dad was being too demanding. I asked her to do the dishes one week, to which she complained that she was made to do all the work while her sister got off scot-free.

She also mentioned how unfair I was. I assertively reaffirmed my request. Caroline scowled but soon acquiesced. The next evening, she took her dishes to the sink, but nothing else. I seized the opportunity to do the three-step praise. I touched her and loudly said, "Great job, Caroline. You remembered to do the dishes tonight." I then said, "I am very proud of you."

Catherine then chimed in. "But Dad, she didn't do anything yet."

I put my finger up to my mouth, hoping Catherine would take the hint and be quiet. Fortunately, Caroline ignored her sister and smiled at me nonetheless.

The Three-Step Reprimand

The other part of the formula is what I call the *three-step reprimand*. The first step is to get your child alone. If you embarrass her in front of her friends or siblings, she will try to sabotage your authority behind your back.

Next, be very specific with your reprimand. Never criticize your child by saying, "Why can't you mind me!" or "What did I just ask you to do?" This is so nonspecific that it creates anxiety. Instead, talk in a soft voice and tell her specifically what she did wrong, such as, "Sweetheart, I have asked you three times to sweep the garage and put away the tools. I won't ask again. I need you to do it now."

Finally, touch your child on the arm or shoulders and tell her how great a job she always does and how proud you are. You will often get excuses as to why she can't obey. Just restate your reprimand and ask again in a loving voice.

This may not be your natural response. You may feel like grabbing a wooden spoon and yelling, "If I have to ask again, I'm going to tan your hide!" But resist your anger, and instead become lovingly assertive. Showing anger with your kids is really an admission that you don't have enough alternatives to deal with the situation.

Also remember to separate the behavior you want to correct from the child's sense of self-worth. Always remember this statement: *correct the behavior, praise the child.* The more consistent you are with this technique, the more you can modify your child's behavior and build self-esteem. If you correct the behavior while praising the child, he will remember the correction while still feeling good about you and the reprimand. When children feel good about their self-worth, they are also prepared to sacrifice to do what they think is right, even when their peers tell them otherwise.

You won't always have to use the three-step praise or reprimand for every occurrence of success or disobedience. In fact, kids need to learn there won't always be someone there to tell them how great a job they have done or to correct them every time there is an infraction. But in the beginning, you need to set patterns of success if you want your kids to develop self-confidence. To do this, get in the habit of praising your kids three to five times each day. Use both the three-step praise and the reprimand. Catch your children in the act of doing things right. Correct them lovingly for those behaviors you want to change.

Do this when your children are young, and you will raise children who accept correction instead of ones who reject and resent you for giving it. You can begin to use these techniques when your kids are teens, but it's much harder then. If you start at an earlier age and stay consistent, you will soon begin to have an impact on their behavior.

Be warned, though: if you get lazy and reprimand more than you praise, your kids will feel manipulated. Their self-esteem will also take a hit. Also, you will eventually be tempted to skip the reprimand and yell just because you are angry. Or you may be tempted to skip the three-step praise when you lack the time to do the whole process. If you let this happen, you will be in the same fix you were in before. You can't teach your kids confidence if you can't model it yourself.

The key is to get kids to engage and do things right because they want to and not to please someone else, like their peer group. This means raising them in a way that causes them to feel good about actions and behaviors that utilize self-confidence.

Here is a good example of some confident and enterprising kids. A police officer found a perfect hiding place for watching speeding motorists. One day, the officer was amazed when everyone was under the speed limit, so he investigated and found the problem. A ten-year-old boy was standing on the side of the road with a huge hand-painted sign that said, "Radar Trap Ahead."

A little more investigative work led the officer to the boy's accomplice: another boy about 100 yards beyond the radar trap with a sign reading "Tips" and a bucket at his feet full of cash.

Be a Good Model

It's easier to develop self-confidence in your kids if you are self-confident. If you tell your three-year-old not to hit the dog, but you give old Rascal a good swat when he steals a piece of bread from the table, you're doomed. Likewise, if you tell your teen to put her clothes away but leave your own clothes lying around the living room, you're setting yourself up for disaster. Every child, every teen, will pounce on a parent who hypocritically asks her to do something yet doesn't do it himself. This is because everything you say and do is a lesson to your kids.

The flip side is also true. Everything you neglect to say or do is also a lesson. All children learn by modeling. What your kids see and hear is also how they will think and behave. As teens mature, there is a point when they seem to completely reject everything about their parents, but even though they won't admit it, they continue to model your behavior. Consequently, your kids need to see you as a role model, not a friend. They have enough friends. They need parents who care enough about them to teach character, values, and morals. The only way they can learn this is to see those attributes in you.

Consider this scenario: Your kids are fighting in the back seat as you drive them to the park to play. You tell them that if they don't stop fighting, you will turn the car around and take them home. They are quiet for a while, but soon start fighting again. You tell them again to stop and the cycle repeats.

What have they learned? To be quiet for thirty seconds while you calm down? That you don't enforce your warnings?

I took my family snow-skiing when they were young. Caroline was arguing in the car with Catherine. I scolded both of them and said if they didn't stop fighting, I would pull the car over and discipline them. Caroline started to cry. I asked her why. She said she couldn't stop fighting and didn't want to get spanked.

In another example, say a teacher tells a student that if she doesn't bring her grades up, she will be kicked off the cheerleading squad. The girl studies hard for a day and then goes back to the same habits that jeopardized her cheerleading. When she is eventually dismissed from the squad, she is outraged, claiming the teacher is unfair and biased against her. Her parents take her side, blaming the teacher and the school instead of making the student accountable for her actions.

It doesn't end there. Years later, a boss tells her subordinate, the former cheerleader, to come to work on time instead of being chronically late. The employee apologizes and promises to be prompt the next day at 8:30 a.m. But at 7:30 a.m. she decides to spend extra time doing her hair and waits until the last minute to make the trek to work. There is an accident on the road, and she is late again.

Wouldn't a confident worker leave twenty minutes ahead of time, making sure she arrived on schedule? Responsibility is a lesson she should have learned as a child. Because a child who is required to consistently clean her room, earn decent grades, and complete her chores knows how to take responsibility for her behavior as an adult.

Time-Outs

Ah, young children. They require a lot of attention. Some of them hit. Some of them have temper tantrums. Some take things that don't belong to them. Some perpetually steal toys from their siblings. Some will perpetually scale any barrier to get into what they're not supposed to. The list could go on forever.

For obvious reasons, not the least of which is keeping parents sane, it's wise to start teaching children confidence and discipline when they're young. One of the most effective ways of doing this is to use time-outs.

Say your child throws a tantrum in front of company. You are angry. But instead of paddling her in front of your friends, you give four-year-old Jessica a time-out.

Experts prescribe time-outs as a way for children to think about their actions and what they did wrong. But they serve an even better purpose: they give the child a chance to gain self-control. Self-control is the beginning of self-confidence. A child who is out of control is irrational and unable to make good choices. A child who is in control is able to evaluate the best way to handle a situation.

You tell young Tyler that you would like him to pick up his toys. At five years of age, he sees that request as on par with writing *War and Peace* in an afternoon. It is impossible, and after a few half-hearted minutes of picking up his toy cars, he breaks down crying and screaming.

What do you do? Coddle him and say he doesn't have to pick up? Tell him you will do it instead? Or immediately give him a time-out and talk to him again when he regains control?

Your child's behavioral breakdowns are designed to test your resolve. Are you willing to allow him to control the situation? Or are you willing to be tough, and follow through with your instructions?

When Caroline was seven years old, she started to scream one morning after I told her to clean her room. I left for work and told her to have it done by the time I arrived home for dinner. When I returned, her room was still a shambles. She wanted to watch a TV program after dinner and started to throw a tantrum when I asked her to clean her room instead. I told her to go to her room for a time-out. She said, "Good, I don't have to clean my room now."

I ignored her remark and waited for seven minutes. After the punishment, I walked into her room, and told her that just because she received a time-out didn't mean she was released from obeying me. She cried again. But this time she realized that getting a time-out, and then also having to do the chore, wasn't worth the bad behavior that got her the time-out in the first place.

Note that time-outs can be tailored to the age of the child. Experts typically recommend one minute for each year of the child's age: a two-year-old would receive a two-minute time-out; a six-year-old would receive a six-minute time-out. Caroline was seven, so her time-out was seven minutes long.

Withholding Privileges

As your child gets a little older, you can add the technique of withholding privileges to your parenting arsenal. For example, if in spite of the three-step praise and three-step reprimand, seven-year-old Tony continues to kick his younger brother, or the dog, whenever he's frustrated, he can systematically lose all the privileges he enjoys. When the hour comes when he's not allowed to watch TV, go outside, play with his trucks, or play with friends, he will have ample time to reflect on the reason why—and to take to heart the necessity of stopping the undesirable behavior.

You must be willing to communicate to your children beforehand what is expected and to make them temporarily unhappy if your expectations are not met. You also need to tell them what will happen. You may think you are showing your children mercy by saving them from consequences now. But you are only teaching them that there are no consequences. They will not be able to avoid consequences when they are out in the real world, and you are not helping them prepare for that world by allowing them to avoid them now.

You may be thinking that it is too harsh holding children to the same consequences adults must submit to. You are right. But you can simulate consequences. If your child breaks another's toy, she can be made to pay for half of it. If your child is late to school or a function, you can take TV time away. The better you can prepare your children for adulthood, the more mature, well-adjusted, and confident they will be when they get there.

Teaching Teens Self-Confidence

Teens are a different beast than young children and without a doubt more challenging. All around them are temptations like truancy, shoplifting, and cheating on tests, or sex, drugs, and alcohol. Consequently, teens need self-confidence today more than ever. The reason they are so difficult to control? Two words: *peer pressure*.

There are two main reasons teens cave into peer pressure:

1. They want to be accepted in a group they respect. Often teens will do anything to gain entry to this group, even engage in an activity they know is wrong, because their peers are hip and parents are embarrassing.

Ironically, a large part of helping your children deal with peer pressure is simply to spend more time with them. I went through a messy divorce in 1988. The lawyer on the other side claimed that I didn't deserve more time with my daughter Stacey other than seeing her every other weekend. He argued that quality time is better than quantity time—isn't it?

Research has shown the opposite. Quantity time is what kids need. Quality is nice, but what they need most is for you to be there. Kids who see a parent only on weekends have many more self-confidence problems than those who have frequent contact. Studies of same-sex marriages without fathers show that children crave a father for the boundaries he can set and the authority he can convey. Moms and dads each contribute toward the development of their kids. If one is absent, the child's development becomes lopsided.

2. Teens cave in to peer pressure because they are unable to stand up for their convictions. They may know something is wrong, but they

don't have the courage or self-confidence to say no, especially when saying yes will gain approval, attention, and love from their friends.

Say a teenage boy is told by his friends that if he doesn't drink with the rest of the guys, he's going to have to find someone else to hang out with. This boy doesn't want to drink and knows it's wrong, but he desperately wants to be a part of the group. Being lonely is no fun. In spite of his better judgment, he begins drinking with them, eventually drinking a lot with them. When the group gets in trouble for their various drunken escapades, he's a part of it.

The Ten-Step Method for Building Self-Confidence in Teens

Is it possible to build self-controlled and confident teens? The following ten-step method can help.

1. **Allow your teen to take responsibility**. Teens are trying to become independent. Give them enough freedom to test their abilities. If they want to procrastinate doing schoolwork until the night before it is due, let them. They will learn to give themselves more time to complete it on their next attempt, especially if you give them consequences for bad grades.

It's tough to see kids go through setbacks, but that is what they are—setbacks and not failures. If you rescue your child without letting him learn from his errors, he will repeat them. There are fewer real-life consequences for a young child who misses a deadline on a show-and-tell than for a high-school senior who misses a deadline on a major project—or possibly even fails a grade because she wasn't held accountable. You won't always be there to rescue your child, so let him learn these important lessons early.

2. **Don't let the mosquitoes get you.** To a teen, everything is a major issue. If you decide to fight every battle, you will lose most of them. Decide which battles are worth suiting up for. If your teen wants to change her hair color, don't make an issue about it. But if she wants to get a tattoo or pierce a body part, take your stand. If your teen wants to stay out until midnight with some friends, evaluate whether she can be trusted to come home on time. If she wants to go out with kids you know are bad, put your foot down.

3. **Make your teen a team player.** The antidote to resisting dangerous temptation is to give teens ever-increasing responsibilities that are consistent with their age and level of maturity. This helps them develop character, morality, values, and self-confidence—the armor they can wear against peer pressure. It enables them to say no when they believe something is wrong and helps them set boundaries. It helps them become assertive in dealing with peers. It allows them to raise their sense of self-worth so they still have a desire to belong. It also helps them stay away from bad kids and look for those who share constructive interests.

It is easy to give up and let your teen do whatever he wants, especially if you are hassled over everything you ask him to do. Nonetheless, make sure your teen has responsibilities in your home for which you hold him accountable. Those tasks can be anything from mowing the lawn to helping with the laundry. Yes, it is easier if you do it yourself, but it won't teach your teen responsibility. Make sure your teen knows he is contributing to the well-being of the family.

4. **Take parenting seriously, not yourself.** You are not the best parent in the world, nor are you the worst. If you care, you can't permanently scar your kids. You also need to know that they don't

want a prison guard for a parent. They want a counselor, often on demand, who coaches but doesn't control. Give your kids as many new experiences as you can, but don't worry about what you are, or aren't doing. If you need to be tough, tell them that your Mr. Hyde persona has taken the place of Dr. Jekyll. They will get the message. And remember to have fun with your kids. They will get the message that they shouldn't be so serious either.

My daughter Stacey once wanted me to appeal to her mother to allow her to go out. She had violated curfew and had been grounded by her mother for the next two weekends. Outraged at the consequence, Stacey very sweetly and innocently asked if I would help. I told her that if it were left to me, I would take away her driving privileges as well. She screamed, "You don't care about me. You don't love me, and you have no idea what I need or want." She added, "I can't believe how mean you are. No other parent treats their kids as bad as you do."

I tried not to smile too visibly, though I wanted to laugh out loud. Instead I said, "I know sweetheart. I am so mean, sometimes I want to give myself a time-out." This didn't make her feel any better, but it did keep me from becoming angry.

One of the toughest phases for single parents is dealing with an adolescent who screams that they are the worst parent in the world. (It's hard enough for those who have a partner to back them up.) You need to stay sane by keeping it light. Don't get angry, and remember, "This too shall pass."

5. **Build up trust**. There isn't a teen out there who doesn't think she deserves more trust from Mom and Dad. The problem is that at one point or another, she has done something to lose that trust. I

once told Catherine to clean her room before she called her friends to play. When I got home from work, her room was a mess and she was spending the night at a friend's house. I was irritated that she hadn't listened to me. So the next day I told her to clean her room, and I watched her do it.

She said, "Dad, why are you watching me?"

I said, "Sweetheart, I want to make sure you do what I tell you to do."

"I can't do it if you watch me. You don't trust me to clean my own room?"

"Nope, you have lost my trust for today. But you can earn it back. In the meantime, there is no TV for the next week until you clean your room first. Then we can start to talk about trust again."

If this seems a little harsh, think of your daughter as a teenager, staying out way past curfew, perhaps until 2:00 a.m. Imagine how you'd feel if she didn't call, and wasn't at the place she said she'd be. Deal with the issue of trust now, and you won't have to cope later with the horrific worry of wondering if your kid is in trouble.

Trust is so important that I recommend you test it frequently in little things when your children are young. If they are trustworthy in the little things, they will be dependable in the big ones. If they lie to you about a small issue, treat it like it's a big one. As they get older, give them increasingly harsh consequences if they lie. If you can't trust your teen, you have opened him up to drug abuse, under-age drinking, sex, and a myriad of other deep pits you want to keep them out of. Most importantly, you will have no choice but to communicate that you can't trust them. Consequently, they will act in an untrustworthy fashion. Build up trust by making them faithful in small things first, and do it when they are young.

6. **Speak their language.** Teens have short attention spans when talking to adults. The last thing they want to hear is some diatribe about how to get better grades, or why they need to dress more conservatively. Learn to speak their language by listening to the way they talk to their peers, then mirror those words. Catherine used the word "whatever" to communicate that she no longer wanted to listen and at the same time disagreed. It was sort of a catchall phrase of displeasure. She pronounced it as two words—"Whatever"— usually with disgust dripping from her voice.

Whenever she stalled on doing her homework and offered excuses, or complained about her sister, I just had to voice that one word, pronouncing it as she did, and she knew exactly what I meant.

When my other daughter wore something I thought inappropriate, I used just one word: "Change." Often I added "please" at the end, but I didn't explain my reasoning or justify it. If Caroline wanted to discuss it more, I was willing to talk as long as it didn't become the foundation for an argument. But I also didn't want to give her any opportunity to challenge me either. One word did it.

7. **Expect good work.** The ethic of doing a good job starts in childhood and is cemented in adolescence. So insist on high standards in whatever your teen does. It is easy for teens to do a halfway job just to get it finished, especially when most parents won't evaluate it anyway. The problem is that teens will extend this lackadaisical effort to other tasks as well. A poor job cleaning the room that is accepted as complete extends to an equally poor job on a report for English class. Expecting high standards of work now will install an ethic in your teens that will last long after they leave you for the adult world.

8. **Fade to black**. As time goes on, your job is to become less of an influence on your teen, not more. You are there to teach them how to make decisions, not make them yourself. You need to become less so they can become more.

In the sitcom *Everybody Loves Raymond*, the family of the grown son moves in across the street and visits without warning, nearly every day. The problem is the mother, a controlling woman who thinks her parenting duties extend throughout life. In one episode, she brings over a cake and insists that Raymond eat it because he looks so skinny that day.

In a similar situation, a mother of a teen girl recently told me that they do everything together, even talk about each other's boyfriends and gossip. That statement made me cringe. The teen needs a parent who helps steer her toward success as an adult, not become her best childhood friend.

It's important to be close to your kids, but not at the expense of being a parent. Friends don't direct or supervise another, nor do they enforce consequences. Friends accept one another without judgment, while a parent is there to judge and correct—exactly what teens need. One bright teen told a group of peers, "I love my mom; we're good friends. But I already have friends. I want a mom."

9. **Make your teen feel loved no matter what happens**. If you're not careful, arguments, fights, and disagreements can turn into feelings of anger and emotional abandonment. Kids frequently feel that if they don't have your approval, they don't have your love. It's important to communicate to them that you will always love them, no matter what happens. The more you say this, the more they will be able to resist peer pressure in their teen years. If you

don't tell them, they may begin looking elsewhere for the love and affection they don't get from you. That leads to teenage pregnancy and other serious issues.

10. **Be consistent**. This is the most important part of building confidence in your teen. Playing tough one day, only to let your child slide the next, is a nightmare of mixed signals. If you prepare your children for consistency as teens, they will show consistency as adults. If you adopt a permissive stance in their teen years, they will display the same later.

The fact remains that you are busy and don't always have a great deal of time to devote to your teen, but consider this scenario. Say a child is raised in a permissive home separated from responsibility and consequences. He is taught that if he doesn't want to do his homework, Mom will talk to the teacher and get an extension. Or if he doesn't want to go to school, Dad will call and get him a day off or write him an excuse.

As a teen, this boy fathers a child and denies it. After breaking a number of hearts, he marries shortly after college but divorces before he is twenty-five. He marries again and has two kids. He argues with his wife because of money and again initiates divorce, this time to marry someone more attractive. He sees his children on occasional weekends but never takes a strong role in their lives. They grow up angry and disillusioned, with numerous problems of their own. The man's new wife also disappoints him. After a third divorce, he marries for a fourth time in his fifties, but soon divorces again because of "irreconcilable differences."

Does this actually happen? Yes, every day, to people you know. We've already talked about the divorce rate for marriages today.

Commitment, duty, and faithfulness are not just Marine Corps slogans. You can teach these lessons to your kids. Start by consistently making them clean their rooms and complete their other chores. Make sure they treat adults with respect. Make sure they get their homework done on time.

Excuses when they're children means unreliability when they're adults. The more you let them slide as children, the tougher things will be years later. The best time for your child or teen to learn self-control and self-confidence is now.

Assignments: Putting Self-Confidence to Work

1. Set up three rules for your children you can enforce consistently. Come up with appropriate consequences. Arriving at the dinner table upon the first request may be nice, but you may not care enough about it to exact punishment if the rule is broken.

   My kids frequently used to be late for school in the morning, so we decided they needed to be in the car by 8:15 or there was no TV time that night. The kids often didn't think about the consequence in the morning, but it really hit them when their favorite programs came on after dinner and they were unable to watch them.

2. Begin using the three-step praise and three-step reprimand techniques on your kids today. Praise them for doing things that are close to being right. Don't wait for them to perform perfectly—this may never happen. Build their self-esteem by praising them for being approximately right.

3. The next time your kids make mistakes, allow them to experience the consequences. If they lie, push them to apologize to the person they dishonored. If they steal, make them replace the article they stole with a similar but better item. If they break an object, make them replace it. Don't protect your kids from experiencing the consequences of their actions, or they will be doomed to repeat the same mistakes over and over again.

In this book you have learned that self-confidence can be learned and taught. You have learned how to set goals and outcomes. You learned how to manage stress, which often the enemy of self-confidence. You have learned how to overcome learned helplessness, and acquire a state of flow, matching your skills with your challenges. You have even learned how to raise self-confident kids.

I recommend you read this book at least five times. I promise you will learn new things on every time through. If you want to contact me through email, it is Kerry@kerryjohnson.com. Twitter is @DrKerryJohnson, and the same for LinkedIn. Good luck in building self-confidence!